THE FANTASY SPORTS BOSS 2018 NFL DRAFT GUIDE

BY MICHAEL E. KENESKI

TABLE OF CONTENTS

EDITOR'S NOTE

To Our Readers:

Yeah, it is that time again. With it being a torturous slog since the confetti fell on Super Bowl 51, the 2018 NFL Draft is almost upon us. The extravaganza that is the draft has become an unofficial three-day holiday for pigskin loyalists and the true beauty of the whole process centers on the sense of optimism/excitement that comes with the arrival of reinforcements. Whether you are the New England Patriots or the Cleveland Browns, the draft ushers in the first glimpses of the 2018 season and the expectations that come with it. New franchise QB's will steer organizations into a new era, while those playoff-established teams sit there believing that one final piece can possibly put them over the top. By the end of the draft, fans of all 32 teams will either be delirious with joy or sick to their stomachs with nausea based on what took place over 7 rounds of picks. And that my friends is why the NFL Draft is such a popular yearly piece of appointment television.

So it is under that premise we present to you our 9th annual Fantasy Sports Boss NFL Draft Guide and this year's installment is once again jam-packed with all the information you need regarding the prospects who stand the best chance of hearing their names called Thursday through Saturday this April. We watched hours upon hours of film of players from all across the country and at various levels of the college football game and our analysis of those included in this book reflect the tendencies/habits that stood out on the screen. As with any draft, there will be surprise stars and also some key busts that will defy all expectations. In the end, though, this is what truly makes the draft such must-see TV. You simply can't ever predict what is going to happen in this ultimate form of unscripted reality television but it sure is fun trying.

Sincerely,

Michael E. Keneski
The Fantasy Sports Boss
ww.thefantasysportsboss.com

2018 NFL DRAFT TEN BURNING QUESTIONS

Outside of our position rankings and analysis, arguably our most popular annual feature in these pages is our "Ten Burning Questions" piece where we delve in on some of the more pertinent issues shaping the draft. As we always say each season in this space, these ten questions and answers only scratch the surface of the draft but most are at the top of the curiosity list for all involved. So with that said, let's start giving the 2018 NFL Draft some more clarity by figuring out these major potential plotlines.

1. Q: Getting the most obvious question out of the way first, who will be the number 1 pick in the 2018 NFL Draft?
A: This is always the million dollar question (or multi-million dollar question for the potential players involved) but this season the answer is far from obvious when you consider that the always unpredictable Cleveland Browns are in the top spot. The Browns have always skipped to their own beat when it comes to the draft and 2018 figures to be no different on that front as they have publicly been connected to QB's Sam Darnold, Josh Rosen, and Josh Allen; plus running back Saquon Barkley. With the Browns having come off a winless season that had the fans picketing outside team headquarters this past December, picking a potential franchise quarterback is the only way to go here. It gets a bit complicated on that front when you consider that UCLA's Rosen has put out word he is not interested in playing for the Browns. Given that bit of potential controversy, look for Darnold to be the pick in a less-noise-is-better situation.

2. Q: Speaking of Rosen and Allen, they won't be waiting long to hear their names called once Darnold is off the board right?
A: Absolutely and especially because there are so many teams at or near the top of the draft that have a pressing quarterback need. Rosen is very much in play for the New York Giants at number 2 and the Indianapolis Colts at three will likely listen to offers from other QB-needy teams such as the New York Jets, Washington Redskins, and Denver Broncos in order to move up and take who the Giants pass on. If we were making a wager, look for Rosen to wear Giants blue and Allen to head to Denver.

3. Q: Baker Mayfield: Trust or Bust?
A: Wow this is going to be an interesting one. Getting past all the off-the-field noise (which is in fact itself a valid red flag to be concerned about), reigning Oklahoma Heisman Trophy-winning QB Baker Mayfield is a true draw-a-line-in-the-sand prospect. If you were to ask 20 different personnel men their opinions on Baker, you would likely see that half would love to draft him and the other half would avoid him like the plague. The fact of the matter is that there are a few worrisome issues with Mayfield that call into question his true prospect standing; with the first being how his 6-1 height will impact his ability to play in the pros. We have seen with similarly-sized Russell Wilson in Seattle and Drew Brees in New Orleans that immense success can be had for players who don't quite fit the height mold and that is a big plus in Mayfield's favor. Instead, we are more concerned about the fact he was exclusively a spread system passer at Oklahoma and historically speaking, there have been quite a few QB busts along the way from the same offensive backgrounds. One only has to look at how brutal Johnny Manziel was in the NFL after he too came from a spread system to know how things can go very wrong with such a history. Then when you add the immaturity issues, Mayfield is as tough a call as you can get

when it comes to any player in the 2018 NFL Draft. In the end, we lean to the side of Mayfield being worth investing in as he played well when the stakes were high in a losing effort in the college championship semifinals and his quick release and very impressive accuracy are tools which often have led to success at the next level.

4. Q: What other QB's could possibly sneak into the first round?
A: One of the more stark NFL Draft trends concern how even some moderate quarterback prospects graduate into the first round despite really possessing ability that is more of the Day 2 or later variety. One only has to look back at the Christian Ponders, Kyle Bollers, and Cade McNowns of the world to serve a reminder of how risky taking such passers can be. It is on that front where Louisville's Lamar Jackson and Oklahoma State's Mason Rudolph reside. Now in terms of physical/athletic attributes, both Jackson and Rudolph are as talented as any quarterback in the entire draft. When it comes to pure passing ability, accuracy, and the reading of defenses, well that is where the trouble starts to arise. Both Jackson and Rudolph have some accuracy troubles and both also need to be schooled on playing from under center (Rudolph) and going through their progressions (Jackson). Buyer beware.

5. Q: Which are the most talent-filled positions in this year's draft?
A: Well quarterback for one has a good collection of potential franchise passers but the other positions that stand out in terms of possessing a high class of skill include offensive tackle, defensive tackle, and especially cornerback.

6. Q: On the flip side, where is the talent lacking in the 2018 NFL Draft?
A: On the offensive side, center and tight end are both quite lean this year. When it comes to the defense, outside linebacker is having a bit of a down year, while middle linebacker and both safety spots are top-heavy.

7. Q: Calvin Ridley or Courtland Sutton?
A: Both Ridley and Sutton are locked-in top 32 picks this April but there are some divergent opinions on who is the better pro prospect. This is of course a splitting hairs exercise since both wideouts are supremely gifted but it comes down to what kind of need at the position a given team is looking for. In Ridley's case, the Alabama star has the better speed and hands. Sutton meanwhile is taller by three inches and is much more capable of being a better red zone target. You really can't go wrong with both but we always prefer the speed/hands advantage over size/physicality.

8. Q: What potential first round picks carry the most bust risk?
A: Trying to figure out which players will go bust is often a futile exercise (after all, if it were so easy, Ryan Leaf, Robert Gallery, and Vernon Gholston would go undrafted) but some players do carry some more inherent risk based on some surface indicators. While we already talked about the risk that Baker Mayfield, Lamar Jackson, and Mason Rudolph bring at QB, some other names that could cause their teams massive headaches include Texas tackle Conor Williams, LSU's defensive tackle Arden Key, and Oklahoma OLB Ogbonnia Okoronkwo. Taking them one at a time, here are the concerning red flags among the three:

Williams: Already having suffered a serious knee injury in 2016, Williams is small for a left tackle at less than 300 pounds. Williams also lacks top-end strength which is a requirement for blocking the outside edge.

Key: Despite possessing a world of natural talent, LSU's junior defensive tackle saw his weight get out of control in 2017 (almost reaching 300 pounds) and Key also has been injured quite a bit. The motor doesn't always go to top speed and the weight issue speaks to a possible lack of discipline.

Okoronkwo: At just 6-1, Okoronkwo is very short for an outside linebacker and he can be neutralized quickly unless he gains the edge. The speed is impressive but Okoronkwo needs to add some more muscle weight this summer.

9. Q: Any possible trades to shake up Round 1?
A: There are always deals to be made when it comes to the NFL Draft and right at the top there could be some big moves. In particular, the Indianapolis Colts could be a target for another team to possibly move up as they already have a franchise QB in Andrew Luck. Under that premise, a team in desperate need at the QB position (New York Jets, Denver Broncos?) need to get on the phone to consummate a move up the board. Also don't overlook the Washington Redskins from making a big move as well since this is Dan Snyder's M.O.

10. Q: How good can Saquon Barkley be?
A: The Penn State running back star is going to be some kind of player as he pretty much checks all of the boxes with regards to being a supreme talent. Think Todd Gurley here as Barkley is very explosive, can score any time he touches the football, and he also is a supreme receiver out of the backfield. Yes the Penn State running back curse is a minor concern but that shouldn't prevent Barkley from being a top five pick.

2018 NFL DRAFT TEAM-BY-TEAM NEEDS

When it comes to the annual NFL Draft, each of the 32 teams involved subscribes to the mantra of taking the best player available in any of the seven rounds they have selections in. This plan of action makes sense when you consider that, not only is there major turnover every season around the league, but the injury rate makes it imperative each team gathers depth at almost every position on the field. Be that as it may, each team will still have some more pressing needs at one spot compared to another and on that front, we present to you the key positions that each NFL franchise will be keying in on this April.

Arizona Cardinals-QB, OT, WR: Larry Fitzgerald can't play forever and so wide receiver should be near the top of the Cardinals' wish lists. Also, the Cardinals are pretty much starting from scratch at the QB position with Carson Palmer retiring and Blaine Gabbert/Drew Stanton showing they are not the answer as a replacement.

Atlanta Falcons-LB, S, TE: A consistent pass-catching tight end should do wonders to help the slipping passing attack get back on track next season. Also, the Falcons need to remedy some slippage both at linebacker and safety.

Baltimore Ravens-WR, OG, CB: Some more depth behind star CB Jimmy Smith would be a help and the Ravens also need to find a big-play wideout to open up the offense more this season.

Buffalo Bills-QB, DT, LB, WR: Nathan Peterman doesn't look to be a good answer in terms of being the future QB and Tyrod Taylor is on a one-way ticket out of town as a free agent. Meanwhile, count on head coach Sean McDermott continuing to mold his defense in the image he envisions and that likely starts with finding a run-stopping defensive tackle.

Carolina Panthers-WR, OT, LB: The Panthers need help at wide receiver after trading Kelvin Benjamin but offensive tackle will likely be at the top of the draft list. Some additional reinforcements are needed at linebacker as well since Luke Kuechly has suffered a bunch of concussions in his career and the next one could be trouble.

Chicago Bears-WR, OT, CB, OG: Mitch Trubisky is the present and future at the QB position for the Bears and they need to surround him with much better receiving talent than the laughable group they had at the position last season. Chicago's offensive line is in need of a massive overhaul as well.

Cincinnati Bengals-LB, DE, OT: Losing Andrew Whitworth at left tackle proved to be a big problem for the Bengals in 2017 and that spot should be the highest priority in April. Alas, the Bengals defense sprung leaks as well due to some of their core guys beginning to age a bit.

Cleveland-QB, RB, CB, S: It is the same story as always with the Browns in that they desperately need to find a franchise QB. Anyone who saw how badly Isaiah Crowell ran the football last season knows that a prime running back is needed as well. Not to be overlooked is the fact the Browns secondary was a joke last season and has been for awhile.

Dallas Cowboys-TE, DT, DE: The end of the line is coming for star tight end Jason Witten and so it makes total sense to get an upstart in here for the future Hall of Famer to tutor. In addition, the Dallas defensive line failed to generate consistent pressure throughout 2017 and that is a big need considering the Cowboys will have to likely go through QB Carson Wentz and their potent passing attack to claim any future NFC East titles.

Denver-QB, OG, OT, CB: Not only was it obvious that the Denver Broncos need a total re-boot at the QB position but they likely are going to cut loose star QB Aqib Talib due to his high salary which makes that spot a major focal point.

Detroit Lions-RB, OT, CB: Other than maybe the Indianapolis Colts, the Lions need a running back more than any other team in the NFL. Some improved play at tackle should also be looked at in order to keep QB Matthew Stafford upright.

Green Bay Packers-WR, CB, OG, DT: It is very possible the Packers are forced to cut loose aging wideout Jordy Nelson and so some fresh blood may be needed at receiver. Also, there can never be enough offensive linemen to help protect QB Aaron Rodgers after seeing how the Packers' season went off the rails when he suffered a broken collarbone last season.

Houston Texans-OT, C, TE: Now that the Texans may finally have their franchise QB in DeShaun Watson, protecting him better with regards to the offensive line becomes very crucial. A consistent pass-catching tight end will also help Watson immensely as the Texans were decimated with injury at the position last season.

Indianapolis-RB, OT, DE: Colts owner Jim Irsay has said publicly he wants a big-time running back in the draft and the men in charge usually get what they want. Like with the Giants, the Colts offensive line has been a perennial problem in desperate need of remediation.

Jacksonville Jaguars-TE, QB, OT, OG: Depending on if Blake Bortles is re-signed or not will determine how the Jaguars handle the QB position in the draft. No matter who is under center though, a pass-catching tight end is sorely needed.

Kansas City Chiefs-CB, LB, DE: The Chiefs defense really let the team down in the second-half collapse versus the Tennessee Titans in the wild-card round last January and the unit overall needs a lot of work. The secondary in particular has become a problem and so a top defensive back should be of "chief" importance.

Los Angeles Rams-OT, CB, LB: With Sean McVay turning the Los Angeles Rams offense into a juggernaut almost overnight, attention will likely turn to the defense in the draft. Specifically speaking, the Rams need to shore up the middle of the defense at middle linebacker and also add another cornerback.

Los Angeles Chargers-QB, OT, S: Philip Rivers is still a very good QB but he is also 37 and not getting any younger. The protection in front of Rivers was pretty miserable at times as well last season.

Miami Dolphins-DE, OG, C, LB: The Dolphin linebacker corps was a major problem spot for them last season and the interior of the offensive line did the various Miami passers no favors either.

Minnesota Vikings-OG, OT, S: The Vikings offensive line was a problem for the second season in a row and grew worse as 2017 went on. This has to be remedied early in the draft and another ball-hawking safety would help as well.

New England Patriots-S, CB, QB: The Patriots secondary was the clear weak link on the defense in 2017 and both safety and cornerback were responsible for surrendering some big passing performances by their opponents. The trade of Jimmy Garoppolo also means the Pats need to get another young QB to develop behind Tom Brady.

New Orleans Saints-LB, QB, WR: Drew Brees can't play forever and so bringing in a young quarterback who can learn for a few seasons is a smart move. The Saints also need a consistent wideout opposite Michael Thomas and on defense, a linebacker boost is overdue.

New York Giants-QB, OT, C, LB: With Eli Manning having turned 37 and the Giants enduring one of the worst seasons in team history, a new franchise QB is very much in the cards. The offensive line was in shambles last season as well and now their best two blockers in Justin Pugh and Weston Richburg are heading toward free agency.

New York Jets-QB, RB, OT, DE: The New York Jets do not have any sort of QB for the future and so that position understandably is at the top of the list. Also by the time you read this, the Jets will have cut Pro Bowl defensive end Muhammad Wilkerson as a result of multiple run-ins with the coaching staff.

Oakland Raiders-LB, DE, S, WR: The Oakland defense is in shambles and new/old head coach Jon Gruden needs to get to work on that unit quickly. Alas, another young wideout should be tabbed as Michael Crabtree is getting a bit up there in age.

Philadelphia Eagles-LT, DE, CB: The secondary remains a work in progress for the Eagles but another defensive tackle should be added to the rotation as well. Of most importance though is the increasing injury issues of LT Jason Peters and that means some major attention needs to be paid to the there.

Pittsburgh Steelers-LB, CB, QB: The Steelers have never met a linebacker prospect they didn't like and so count on them making the position front-and-center in the draft. Like with Eli Manning and Philip Rivers from the same hallowed draft class, QB Ben Roethlisberger can see retirement getting closer.

San Francisco 49ers-OT, WR, CB, RB: With Jimmy Garoppolo now entrenched as the 49ers' QB; they need to give him some more receiving toys to work with. While Marquise Goodwin emerged nicely last season, he needs some help on the other side. Also, Garoppolo got hit way too often when under center last season and so the 49er front office needs to improve the protection in order to keep him on the field.

Seattle Seahawks-OG, OT, CB, S: The Seattle offensive line is a complete joke and they are really playing with fire in terms of risking injury for QB Russell Wilson. Alas, the secondary is aging and becoming more injury-prone by the year which means some new legs are needed there.

Tampa Bay Buccaneers-CB, S, DE, DT: It should be all defense for the Buccaneers in this year's draft as that unit was simply brutal in 2017. Things should start off in the secondary which was burned all throughout last season and operates in a division with some big-time passers.

Tennessee Titans-OG, DE, WR: Eric Decker has not worked out at wideout and the interior of the offensive line was like a turnstile in the divisional round loss to the New England Patriots. The Titans also need to beef up the pass rush which was way too dormant at times last season.

Washington Redskins-QB, WR, LB: The Redskins' draft will take shape once they figure out what they are doing with Kirk Cousins at QB. If they let Cousins walk, finding a new franchise passer becomes their top priority in the draft. Washington also is overdue when it comes to drafting a top wideout.

CAN PENN STATE SUPERSTAR RUNNING BACK SAQUON BARKLEY REVERSE THE SCHOOL'S RUNNING BACK CURSE?

When it comes to the annual extravaganza that is the NFL Draft, the first hour of the proceedings (which encompass the initial 5-6 selections) are almost always dominated by the quarterback fraternity. With the teams picking at the top having endured brutal results/campaigns the year prior, the savior that is the potential franchise QB takes center stage right at the top. While this premise has stayed true almost from the beginning of the drafts inception, some exceptions are made from year-to-year with regard to can't miss prospects from another position being under consideration. In addition to quarterback, transcending offensive tackles, pass rushing defensive ends, the occasional superstar wide receiver, and the shutdown cornerback have made their push into the top tier of the draft as well. And in even more rare instances, an explosive running back comes around among the first few picks every so often and that is certainly the case this time around for the 2018 NFL Draft.

So while QB's Sam Darnold, Josh Rosen, and Jake Allen will all figure prominently right at the top, some room has to be made for Penn State superstar running back Saquon Barkley as well. One only has to watch a few snaps from Penn State's 2017 campaign to see that Barkley is worth every bit an early round draft pick this season given his breathtaking speed, ridiculous cutting ability, well above-average receiving skills, and possessing a home run acceleration that make any touch a potential touchdown. So while on skill alone Barkley looks like the latest in a recent string of top-end running back talent to make it to the NFL as a high draft pick (Ezekiel Elliott, Todd Gurley, Melvin Gordon), there is the one small (or giant) matter regarding the school the kid attended and the not-so-impressive history the Nittany Lions have had when it comes to sending running backs to the NFL. Just mentioning these names is enough to elicit gag reflexes both from their former teams and the NFL fans who once greeted their arrivals as high first-round picks with much excitement; only to be seriously letdown as these careers quickly went down the toilet. Whether it was Ki-Jana Carter (first in 1995), Curtis Enis (5th overall in 1998), or Blair Thomas (second overall in 1990), Penn State has not exactly been Running Back U when it comes to the "can't miss" stars of the position. While some Penn State apologists will throw out Larry Johnson (27th overall in 2003) to refute this, the fact of the matter is that the former Kansas City Chiefs veteran had only two impressive (and yes they were very impressive) campaigns in an 11-year NFL career. In fact, Johnson was so bad his first two years in the league that the Chiefs almost released him outright prior to his back-to-back 1,700-yard seasons from 2005-2006. After that flurry, however, Johnson never rushed for 1,000 yards again and only one time went for over 600 in from 2007 through 2011.

Of course, this journey down a very forgettable draft road for Penn State running backs could be just a futile exercise. After all, the common denominator in those previous running back drafts busts was head coach Joe Paterno. It is entirely possible that Paterno's offensive system was terrific for his running backs on the collegiate level but a zero when it came to the pro game. And as far as Barkley is concerned, the Nittany Lions have employed an NFL-style offense first under Bill O'Brien and now James Franklin since Paterno passed away. Thus, it is grossly unfair to saddle Barkley with the stigma that Penn State sends nothing but high-cost running back draft busts to the NFL and it certainly should not behoove any team (the Indianapolis Colts at number 3???) to select this potential seismic talent.

In the end, Saquon Barkley will have to answer the bust question like every other prospect who hears his name called during the seven rounds of the 2018 NFL Draft. While there inevitably will be some more prime draft busts along the way at any given position, there is also an equal chance that a superstar player will be unveiled. Will that superstar be Barkley? Count this peanut stand as liking his chances.

2018 NFL MOCK DRAFT

As we always do in this space at this time of the year, our annual Mock Draft is an exercise both in strategic selecting; with a heavy dose of guesswork as well given the extreme secrecy of the proceedings leading up to the big day. That still won't stop us from trying to predict how the first 32 picks will go and so barring any trades, this is our best attempt at figuring out what could take place in Round 1.

1. Cleveland-Sam Darnold QB (USC): While there have been reports that Josh Allen could be the guy, can't see the Browns passing on the higher ceiling of USC's Sam Darnold. Maybe now Cleveland finally has their franchise passer.

2. New York Giants-Josh Rosen QB (UCLA): Yes Rosen is a bit of a hot dog and could find some trouble in the big city, the fact of the matter is that he has the pizzazz and skills to be a star in New York. The Giants will not allow a prime opportunity to draft a QB to pass them by given how ugly 2017 was and the best part is that Rosen very much wants to come to town.

3. Indianapolis Colts-Saquon Barkley RB (Penn State): With the Colts letting Frank Gore walk in free agency and owner Jim Irsay saying publicly he wants a superstar back, enter the explosive Barkley to fill that void nicely.

4. Cleveland-Mike McGlinchey OT (Notre Dame): The Browns got their franchise QB in Sam Darnold and now they have to surround him with a stud tackle which they more than an accomplish with Notre Dame's McGlinchey.

5. Denver Broncos-Josh Allen QB (Wyoming): GM John Elway has openly expressed how frustrated he is about the team's miserable QB situation and short of coming out of retirement; the strong-armed Allen is the right call here.

6. New York Jets-Baker Mayfield QB (Oklahoma): The New York Jets have nothing in the cupboard at QB since Christian Hackenberg and Bryce Petty both turned out to be monstrous busts and so Oklahoma's Baker Mayfield almost has to be the pick here. While there are questions about Mayfield's size and maturity, he also seems to have the "It" factor to succeed in the bright lights of New York.

7. Tampa Bay Buccaneers-Minkah Fitzpatrick CB (Alabama): This one is too obvious not to happen as the Buc's were a sieve in their secondary last season. Enter the best do-everything cornerback to come out in years in Alabama's Minkah Fitzpatrick.

8. Chicago Bears-Calvin Ridley WR (Alabama): The Bears had arguably the worst batch of wideouts in the NFL last season and it is imperative they give QB Mitch Trubisky some more offensive weapons to speed up his development.

9. San Francisco 49ers-Conor Williams OT (Texas): The 49ers could go wideout or cornerback here but protecting new franchise QB Jimmy Garoppolo is almost high on their priority list.

10. Oakland Raiders-Roquan Smith ILB-Georgia: This is a big need for the Raiders as the defense behind Khalil Mack was pathetic all of last season. Smith is a tackling machine who can be a Pro Bowler right out of the gate.

11. Miami Dolphins-Quenton Nelson OG (Notre Dame): The Dolphins seriously need to address the offensive line which has gotten their quarterbacks killed the last two seasons. While they could go tackle, the best guard in the draft in Notre Dame's Quenton Nelson should be just as good of an upgrade.

12. Cincinnati Bengals-Bradley Chubb DE N.C. State: With Marvin Lewis back in the fold for 2018, look for the defensive coach to retool his unit with the best pass rusher in the draft.

13. Washington Redskins-Orlando Brown OT (Oklahoma): Yes they need a QB but the Redskins also need to rebuild a sagging O-line that has an aging and increasingly injured Trent Williams on it.

14. Green Bay Packers-Courtland Sutton WR (SMU): The Packers are likely going to be moving on from aging/injury-prone wideout Jordy Nelson this winter and so SMU's Courtland Sutton could immediately be a very capable replacement.

15. Arizona Cardinals-Mason Rudolph QB (Oklahoma State): It may be a stretch for Oklahoma State's Rudolph to crack the first round of the draft but this is what always happens when there are a high number of QB-needy teams as there are this season. After all Christian Ponder and Cade McNown were both once first rounder's as well.

16. Baltimore Ravens-Marcus Davenport DE (UTSA): The strength of the Baltimore Ravens defense is their secondary and the pass rush needs infusion as Terrell Suggs is not going to be around forever.

17. Los Angeles Chargers-Kolton Miller OT (UCLA): The Chargers stay in-state for a supreme potential franchise tackle to extend the career of QB Philip Rivers a bit longer.

18. Seattle Seahawks-Ogbonnia Okoronkwo LB (Oklahoma): One only had to look at how the Los Angeles Rams humiliated the Seattle defense last season to know that some changes need to be made here.

19. Dallas Cowboys-Derwin James S (Florida State): The Cowboys could look at Courtland Sutton to help the inconsistent wideout corps but the secondary also needs a big help as well.

20. Detroit Lions-Derrius Guice RB (LSU): The Lions are already talking about how they want to take a running back in the draft and LSU's Guice is the best option once we see Saquon Barkley come off the board.

21. Buffalo Bills-Tremaine Edwards LB (Virginia Tech): Count on McDermott doubling up on the defensive side as he continues to make the Bills over in his image.

22. Buffalo Bills-Maurice Hurst DT (Michigan): Sean McDermott is a defensive coach and he couldn't have been happy seeing his team gets gashed up the middle they way they did for almost all of last season.

23. Los Angeles Rams-Christian Kirk WR (Texas A @ M): Just think what had coach Sean McVay may have up his sleeves once he gets a hold of this speedy, big-play wideout.

24. Carolina Panthers-Denzel Ward CB (Ohio State): The Panthers are still trying to find Josh Norman's replacement and they have a good chance of doing so with the solid coverage skills of the Buckeye's Ward.

25. Tennessee Titans-Joshua Jackson CB (Iowa): The Titans will see Andrew Luck, DeShaun Watson, and the improved Blake Bortles come back into the division next season which makes fixing their leaking secondary a must.

26. Atlanta Falcons-Rashaan Evans LB (Alabama): The NFC South remains a pass-heavy league and so defense should once again be a high priority for head coach Dan Quinn.

27. New Orleans Saints-Malik Jefferson LB (Texas): The Saints have made some nice headway on their previously anemic yearly defenses by fixing the secondary. Now they need to get to work on the shaky linebacker corps.

28. Pittsburgh Steelers-Harrison Phillips DT (Stanford): The Steelers were a bit soft up the middle last season and plugging in the beefy Phillips should remedy that in a hurry.

29. Jacksonville Jaguars-James Washington WR (Oklahoma State): With Allen Robinson and Marqise Lee both free agents, the Jags re-tool with the supremely talented and very athletic Washington.

30. Philadelphia Eagles-Chukwuma Okorafor OT (Western Michigan): The pass protection was a disgrace for the Philadelphia Eagles last season and it cost him a possible Super Bowl championship once QB Carson Wentz went down. Not again.

31. Minnesota Vikings-Lamar Jackson QB (Louisville): Whether they bring back Case Keenum or not, Vikes head coach Mike Zimmer will have a longer-term strategy for the QB position. Jackson would be able to learn for a season or two behind Keenum and protect the Vikings in case the latter goes back to the struggles from the earlier stage of his career.

32. New England Patriots-Vita Vea DT (Washington): Count on Bill Belichick to continue tinkering with the defense as that is where his roots lie.

So there you have it. Of course so much can change from this point forward in terms of trades, free agency, and other issues that could make this mock looks silly but no one ever really has the answers as to what any team will do. After all, if we had that information, what fun would the draft be anyways?

POSITION RANKINGS AND ANALYSIS

*Denotes underclassmen

QUARTERBACKS

Position Grade: A-

First Round Talent: Josh Rosen, Sam Darnold, Josh Allen, Baker Mayfield

*Josh Rosen (UCLA) 6-4 210 4.75: Having passed USC's Sam Darnold as the consensus top quarterback in the 2018 NFL Draft, the only thing left up for debate is whether or not UCLA's Josh Rosen would accept playing for the Cleveland Browns if the organization makes him the number 1 pick. Evoking memories of Eli Manning stating publicly that he didn't want to play for the San Diego Chargers (who held the top pick in his draft class), Rosen has publicly hinted the same feelings for the Browns which bear watching. With that said, Rosen is a supreme talent who possesses all the tools necessary to be a franchise quarterback for whichever team he ends up with. While he can be a bit brash and a tad more outspoken than you like, Rosen has impeccable throwing mechanics which help him unleash a tight spiral almost every time he drops back. Blessed with a cannon for an arm, there is no throw or window that Rosen can't exploit. It does need to be said however that Rosen is not the most durable quarterback and that lend some risk to the draft equation. Also, Rosen carried the reputation for being a bit of a prima donna as well. In the end, though, you are looking at a future Pro Bowl gunslinger.

*Sam Darnold (USC) 6-4 225 4.78: While he did cede to Josh Rosen the mantle of being the consensus top quarterback in the 2018 NFL Draft, USC's Sam Darnold is an unbelievable franchise-caliber talent in his own right. Yes, Darnold had a better sophomore campaign than he did as a junior last season but the tools are all evident here. Primarily speaking, Darnold has excellent accuracy and that is a crucial trait for a passer that can't really be taught. Almost every NFL executive would tell you they would rather have an accurate QB with an average arm than one with a cannon and no touch. Darnold possesses both accuracy and arm strength however and that makes him a sure-fire top-five pick this coming May. What you really have to love about Darnold is how he anticipates routes and throws the football where his receiver can continue running once he secures the catch. Unfortunately, Darnold does tend to lock in on his target and that can lead to interceptions. Darnold also needs to get to work on his ball security as he reminds many of Kurt Warner in how he is prone to fumbling. While you would love to be compared to Kurt Warner overall, drawing similarities to the Hall of Famer's annual fumbling problem is the one thing you don't wish to be associated with as a QB prospect. Yes, the hype has cooled just a bit compared to last season but Darnold can do a nice Andrew Luck impersonation if he irons out the turnovers.

*Josh Allen (Wyoming) 6-4 222 4.75: Blessed with an NFL quarterbacking body and arm, Wyoming's Josh Allen is an intriguing prospect who will likely hear his name called among the top 15 picks. Unlike Josh Rosen and Sam Darnold however, Allen is a bit of a work in progress who will likely need to sit initially during his rookie season. That is because, for all of Allen's arm strength and underrated athleticism, the accuracy leaves quite a bit to be desired as he completed just 56 percent of his passes in 2017. This is a bit scary as accuracy can be very tough to teach and the fear is that Allen could be another Kyle Boller or Byron Leftwich who both struggled badly in that area in going bust at the next level. This one could go either way.

Baker Mayfield (Oklahoma) 6-2 214 4.71: Boy, there may not be a more polarizing player in the entire 2018 NFL Draft. First off, let's dispense with the idea that Baker Mayfield won't be a first-round pick as he most certainly will be considering the collegiate numbers and the fact that top QB prospects always tend to push into the top 32 picks by the time the proceedings get underway. When it comes to Mayfield, his numbers were just stupid good at Oklahoma as he laid claim to the 2017 Heisman Trophy. The question is whether or not Mayfield is a product of the spread system employed in Oklahoma and also whether or not his 6-1 height will be a hindrance as a pro. Each are valid concerns but perhaps most troubling is Mayfield's propensity for getting into trouble both on and off the field. Those troubles include an arrest for public intoxication, fleeing the police, and resisting arrest. Mayfield also caught much-deserved flak for grabbing his crotch while uttering an obscenity at the Kansas bench (to which he was stripped of the captaincy for his final regular season game) and also for planting the Sooners flag in the middle of the Ohio State logo during a game last September. With memories of Ryan Leaf and Johnny Manziel still haunting many an NFL executive, there will surely be some who take Mayfield off their draft boards given the character questions. Now getting back to the tools, Mayfield has excellent accuracy and the ability to throw a catchable ball consistently. Comparisons to Russell Wilson are understandable on those fronts. What he does lack is arm strength to make plays at a high rate down the field; while also showing some shoddy footwork in the pocket. When you combine that with the personality issues, Mayfield looks to be too radioactive a prospect to be worth investing a high draft choice in. Is he Wilson or Manziel? That will be the ultimate debate for whoever thinks of drafting Mayfield this spring.

Lamar Jackson (Louisville) 6-6-3 205 4.57: Former Heisman Trophy winning QB Lamar Jackson put up some ridiculous numbers while at Louisville but his NFL prospects are all over the map depending on whom you speak to. On the positive side, Jackson has breathtaking speed and athleticism for the position. Capable of buying time in the pocket or taking off on a run, Jackson needs to be accounted for at all times given that speed. What really makes Jackson stand out as a prospect as well is the fact he complements his running ability with a powerful arm that can make all the throws in eliciting some Michael Vick comparisons. The Vick talk is spot on too when it comes to Jackson's issues with overall accuracy and reading defenses. Jackson often runs at the first sign of trouble and not in the Russell Wilson way in terms of buying time for his receivers to get open. With regards to accuracy, Jackson completed just 56 and 60 percent of his throws the last two years which speak to some struggles there. Keep in mind though that DeShaun Watson was dogged with accuracy questions coming into the draft last year as well and all he did was light the NFL on fire as a rookie a year ago before suffering a torn ACL. At the very least, Jackson carries loads of potential as a franchise-type QB who can beat opposing defenses both through the air and on the ground.

Mason Rudolph (Oklahoma State) 6-5 235 4.85: It can be tough to grade Oklahoma State QB Mason Rudolph due to the simplistic offense he has run at the collegiate level and things become murkier when you turn on the tape. It is there where Rudolph's accuracy issues become apparent and he also has struggled to place the football where his receivers can run after the catch. Rudolph also operated almost exclusively out of the shotgun at OSU and that will need some coaching at the next level as well to break the habit. The size and strength are impressive though and Rudolph can physically take an NFL pounding which is an underrated ingredient to possess. While ideally, you would like Rudolph to get a year of watching/learning under his belt, he figures to be drafted prominently given his classic NFL frame and arm strength.

Luke Falk (Washington State) 6-4 205 4.79: Yet another QB sleeper who could be a diamond in the rough, Washington State's Luke Falk grades out nicely in the accuracy department. Falk also pairs the accuracy with solid arm strength that can make most NFL throws. What is not so attractive is the fact Falk faces a learning curve at the NFL level after operating almost exclusively out of the shotgun at Washington State. Falk also is very thin and could be looking at injury problems unless he adds weight/strength. A project worth taking on.

Riley Ferguson (Memphis) 6-4 210 4.83: Has to deal with following in the footsteps of Paxton Lynch who has been a gigantic bust so far in the NFL. The problem is that the system in Memphis is not NFL-friendly and Ferguson has some of the same issues that Lynch struggled with such as shaky accuracy and a tendency to lock in on his first read. Ferguson is also very slight in his frame which is another red flag in terms of holding up to an NFL rush.

Logan Woodside (Toledo) 6-2 201 4.75: While his college career couldn't have ended any worse in tossing 3 interceptions versus Appalachian State in the Dollar General Bowl, Toledo QB Logan Woodside has a chance to be a late-round pick given his powerful arm and above-average accuracy. When it comes to the accuracy, NFL personnel execs will always lean toward those prospects over erratic power-armed guys since the former skill can't really be taught. Of course, as the bowl game showed, Woodside is turnover prone and gets a bit too confident he can slide the football into any opening.

Nick Stevens (Colorado State) 6-3 190 4.70: Having put up some terrific numbers as a senior for Colorado State, QB Nick Stevens has a chance to hear his name called in the seventh round of the 2018 NFL Draft. That is as high as the draft ceiling will go here however as Stevens is incredibly skinny and will have a very tough time holding up against an NFL rush. What Stevens does have going for him are a quick release and good ball placement. That will not likely be enough though to improve his stock much at all and there is just as good a chance Stevens goes completely undrafted.

*Tanner Lee (Nebraska) 6-4 220 4.74: A surprise early QB entrant into the 2018 NFL Draft was surely Nebraska QB Tanner Lee who posted just a mediocre 23/16 ratio when it came to touchdowns/INT's last season. The real reason for the move centered on the fact Lee was a terrible fit as a stationary pocket passer in new head coach Scott Frosts' offense. Considering that Frost was a tremendous option QB during his Nebraska days and one can now understand why Lee made the jump. Whatever the reason, Lee is likely destined to be a day three selection as he is mistake-prone and may be a sitting duck in the pocket for NFL defensive lineman. Lee does possess a professional arm that can make almost all the throws though and so as a project player you can do a lot worse.

Jarret Stidham (Auburn) 6-3 210 4.72: Highly accurate passer who has good but not great arm strength and above-average touch. Stidham made his way to Auburn after leaving scandal-plagued Baylor and steadily improved throughout his run in the SEC cauldron. While a bit on the short side, Stidham's positives in the accuracy department and comfort in the pocket make him a solid developmental prospect.

Kurt Benkert (Virginia) 6-4 215 4.79: Another spread system QB who needs to get to work on taking snaps from under center is Virginia senior Kurt Benkert. Benkert checks out both in the size and strength columns but the issues begin to crop up when focusing in on his lack of pocket awareness. Took some big hits during his Virginia career which speaks to not adequately sensing the rush and Benkert also is not adept at going through his reads. What Benkert does well is throw a nice deep ball and he has the mobility to keep the play alive while continuing to look down the field.

THE REST

Alex McGough (Florida International) 6-2 220 4.74

Mike White (Western Kentucky) 6-4 225 4.79

Ryan Finley (N.C. State) 6-4 205 4.82

Nic Shimonek (Texas Tech) 6-3 225 4.81

Jake Browning (Washington) 6-2 205 4.73

Kenny Hill (TCU) 6-1 205 4.73

Trace McSorley (Penn State) 6-0 195 4.79

Quinton Flowers (South Florida) 6-0 210 4.60

Kyle Allen (Houston) 6-3 210 4.74

Richard Lagow (Indiana) 6-6 240 4.83

RUNNING BACKS

Position Grade: B+

First Round Talent: Saquon Barkley, Nick Chubb, Darius Guice

***Saquon Barkley (Penn State) 5-11 223 4.49:** Introducing the next great NFL running back prospect. Grading out as high as any running back to come out in the last ten years, Penn State's explosive Saquon Barkley won't hang around long in the 2018 NFL Draft. Barkley pretty much checks all of the boxes as he has tremendous instant acceleration and speed through the hole. In addition, Barkley has excellent balance and the speed to take it out on the edge and quickly get up the field. As great a runner as Barkley is, he also is a phenomenal receiver out of the backfield and profiles similar to the Los Angeles Rams' Todd Gurley. About the only issue that would give one pause regarding Barkley is the brutal history of Penn State running backs, which is a fraternity of lowlights including Blair Thomas, Ki-Jana Carter, and Curtis Enis.

***Derrius Guice (LSU) 5-11 212 4.52:** Understudy to Leonard Fournette early in his LSU career, speedy junior Derrius Guice showed in 2017 that he was up to being a starter for the Tigers in picking up 1,153 rushing yards and 11 touchdowns. While he dealt with a knee injury during the year, Guice didn't let it impact him late in the season. Runs a bit hot-and-cold in the passing game but the upside is sizable.

***Bryce Love (Stanford) 5-10 196 4.50:** Not only is Bryce Love a high-end brainiac (having majored in medicine), the Stanford running back can play football at a pretty darn good level as well. In a 2017 season that got him an invite to the Heisman Trophy ceremony, Love rushed for a whopping 2,118 yards at an 8.1 clip while scoring 19 touchdowns on the ground. In terms of the running game, Love has a compact frame and high-end quickness to pile up the yards in a hurry. Love is a bit one-dimensional though as he caught just 6 passes last season and thus, will likely come out on third downs at the NFL level. While clearly a notch or two below Saquon Barkley, Love grades out as a late first round or early second round pick.

Sony Michel (Georgia) 5-11 212 4.49: The other half of the very effective running back duo with Nick Chubb on the 2017 Georgia Bulldogs, Sony Michel has earned plaudits from NFL front office executives due to his impressive speed and ability to help in the passing game. While he doesn't have the power of Chubb, Michel can make defenders miss with his ability to stop on a dime and juke his way into the open field. Boy did Michel show those skills in the college football semis when he ran all over Oklahoma in rushing for 4 scores. Major upside pla whose lack of top-end carries in college masks the potential.

Nick Chubb (Georgia) 5-10 220 4.51: Georgia's Nick Chubb is an extremely productive speedster who followed in the Todd Gurley footsteps with the Bulldogs. It was a bit of an up-and-down career at Georgia for Chubb as he once looked like a can't miss star in 2015 before a serious knee injury led to a disappointing 2016 campaign. Last season though, Chubb looked like his old 2015 version and so he has positive momentum heading into the draft. Chubb is a b of a question mark in terms of how good he really can be due to the fact Georgia didn't lean on him heavily due to their depth and he was virtually useless in the passing game. As far as running was concerned, however, Chubb more than makes the grade there since he has excellent vision, cutting ability, and acceleration. Similar to Bryce Love, Chubb will likely work in tandem at the NFL level with a pass-catching back.

*Ronald Jones (USC) 6-0 200 4.55: Likely benefitting from defenses focusing in on Sam Darnold, USC's Ronald Jones still flashed impressive agility and a speed-oriented running game. While he could use a bit more weight on his frame, Jones was able to pick up yardage in tight and also break to the outside when needed. Improvement in his receiving skills is needed however if Jones wants to be an every-down player.

Royce Freeman (Oregon) 5-11 230 4.56: A big back who can run over defenders. Royce Freeman has been a heavily-worked running back for the Oregon Ducks the last two seasons and he has responded with big numbers such as the 1,475 yards and 14 touchdowns in 2017. While the collegiate numbers are eye-opening, Freeman is quite limited in terms of his pro outlook. For one thing, Freeman does not catch the football and he has little in the way of agility to the outside. Likely will have to settle for the power portion of a tandem at the NFL level.

*Kerryon Johnson (Auburn) 6-0 212 4.54: Bigger power back who is mostly a north-south runner but a good one at that. Johnson has the impressive speed for his size and he drives forward with good force to pick up additional yards after contact. Doesn't have to come out on third downs as well since Johnson has the decent hands to help in the passing game. A bit under the radar going into the draft, Johnson looks like a nice value.

*Josh Adams (Notre Dame) 6-2 225 4.57: Thought Adams should have stayed in school for another year but he had a nice 2017 campaign in serving as a powerful north-south runner for the Irish. Able to take advantage of the giant holes opened by the phenomenal Notre Dame O-line to power through defenses and Adams did a nice job continually moving forward upon contact given his immense frame. Has goal-line back written all over him with regards to Adams' potential NFL impact.

Damien Harris (Alabama) 5-11 214 4.53: Worked in tandem with Bo Scarborough to give the Crimson Tide another very impressive running game. Harries grades out higher than Scarborough in terms of being an NFL prospect due to the fact he has more explosiveness and is a solid receiver. Also has shown the toughness and leg drive to add yardage upon contact.

Akrum Wadley (Iowa) 5-11 191 4.50: Earning more plaudits for his return and pass receiving game than what he has done running the football, Iowa's Akrum Wadley seems set to be part of a committee at the NFL level. Can step right in and be the receiving back on third down in such an arrangement but Wadley's 4.4 yards per carry as a senior and lack of size are negatives.

*L.J. Scott (Michigan State) 6-1 230 4.56: While Scott saw his rushing numbers dip a bit compared to 2016, you can easily make the case that the Michigan State back improved as an NFL prospect almost across the board last season. For one thing, Scott began to contribute in the passing game for the first time with 20 receptions and he also showed underrated agility and quickness despite his power running frame. Clearly, Scott has the size and heft to pick up the tough yardage but he has some speed as well.

Rashaad Penny (San Diego State) 5-11 220 4.61: The quality of competition faced each week could call into question the totality of the numbers achieved by San Diego State's Rashaad Penny but that would be unfair to a point. Penney has excellent quickness and vision to help him always churn forward for yardage and he runs with fierce power in relishing contact. On the negative side, Penny mostly is a one-cut runner who does need to play with a lower pad level so as not to get undercut. Not a flashy player by any means but Penny could work nicely in a tandem with a speedier compliment.

Martez Carter (Grambling State) 5-9 205 4.51: Small school scatback who has explosive speed and the ability to score every time he touches the football. Will likely be slated for a Darren Sproles-like role at the NFL level in that Carter is a tremendous receiver for a running back and when utilized in space, can make some big plays. Won't be able to consistently be a runner however given the durability concerns and utter lack of size but there are tools to work with here. Speed like this will always have a place on an NFL roster no matter what school such a player comes from.

*Bo Scarborough (Alabama) 6-2 228 4.54: The conveyer belt of running backs coming from Alabama into the NFL shows no sign of slowing down as both Bo Scarborough and Damien Harris will join a recent fraternity that includes Mark Ingram, Eddie Lacy, Trent Richardson, and T.J. Yeldon. As far as Scarborough is concerned, he served as the power complement to Harris' speed last season for the Tide and did a nice job in rushing for 549 yards and 8 scores at 5.1 a pop. Scarborough is a true power back in every sense of the word as he lacks the speed to get outside consistently and is more apt to run over defenders in a north-south manner. The depth in the Tide backfield though kept Scarborough from showing his full potential and that will make him quite attractive once the draft rolls around. For instance, Scarborough has decent receiving ability but he was not asked to do much of that for Alabama. He also has the frame to be a true workhorse back and could yield some significant draft value on those traits alone.

Ito Smith (Southern Miss) 5-9 195 4.42: Southern Miss running back Ito Smith is a classic example of what should be a late-round pick who could quickly become a big NFL contributor solely due to his massive speed. Having reportedly been clocked as fast as an insane 4.40 in the 40-yard dash, Smith can quickly work his way into a speed portion of a committee at the next level. Of course, Smith's very slight frame caps what can only be a modest amount of work each week but speed will always be in demand among NFL personnel gurus.

*Mike Weber (Ohio State) 5-10 212 4.55: An early hamstring injury cost Mike Weber the starting running back job for the Ohio State Buckeyes for 2017 but that shouldn't completely overshadow the talent that allowed him to rush for 1,096 yards and 9 scores in 2016 replacing Ezekiel Elliott. It is almost advised to give Weber a mulligan on last season as he was never truly right physically and thus, unable to showcase the solid running/receiving game that elicited some Elliott comparisons the year prior. While certainly not as fast and explosive as Elliott, Weber can shake tackles and has a decent array of moves to get him into the open field. Weber also has a decent set of hands to help in the passing game as well. Untapped potential is the word here.

Kyle Hicks (TCU) 5-10 210 4.53: While he did not flash much as a runner, TCU's Kyle Hicks has terrific receiving ability that has drawn comparisons to the New Orleans Saints' Alvin Kamara. That is some comparison and truth be told, Kamara was a bit off the draft radar as a third-round pick with a similar offensive profile to Hicks. Hicks is an excellent route runner like Kamara and has soft hands to make even difficult catches. Could easily make it as a third down back and be a solid weapon on that side of the offensive attack.

*Myles Gaskin (Washington) 5-10 193 4.52: Despite being a bit on the short side, Washington's Myles Gaskin is a big play waiting to happen given his instant acceleration and top-end speed. Flashing both as a runner and a receiver, Gaskin can help all over the field. Gaskin's junior season was straight out of a video game as he rushed for 1,282 yards and 19 touchdowns while adding 18 catches for another 228 yards and 3 more scores. While he may need to be capped in terms of carries per game given his lack of size, Gaskin looks like a mid-round potential gem.

Ralph Webb (Vanderbilt) 5-10 202 4.48: A Rotational back who could help as a returner and a speedster who gets 5-7 carries a game; while also operating on third down. Webb struggled as a pure runner with Vanderbilt given his lack of size. Often going down on the first contact, Webb was too much of an all-or-nothing runner.

Roc Thomas (Jacksonville State) 5-11 193 4.55: A kid who slipped through the cracks, Jacksonville State's Roc Thomas has a cool name and an intriguing game. While Thomas did begin his collegiate career at Auburn, he transferred to Jacksonville State for a better chance to play and it paid off as he rushed for 1,065 yards and 13 scores at 6.0 per carry as a senior. What is interesting is that Thomas' tape doesn't pop on any front but he looks like a sum-of-all-parts prospect.

Justin Jackson (Northwestern) 5-11 193 4.55: Northwestern's Justin Jackson is another senior running back who does his best work in the receiving game. While not lauded as an impact runner during his collegiate days, Jackson also did his best while operating behind a brutal O-line. The speed is decent enough here but Jackson fails to consistently make defenders miss and fight through contact. He will make his way as a pro mostly as a receiving back and not much else.

THE REST

Kalen Ballage (Arizona State) 6-3 230 4.53

Lavon Coleman (Washington) 5-11 228 4.59

*Kamryn Pettway (Auburn) 6-0 235 4.58

*Travon McMillan (Virginia Tech) 6-0 200 4.57

Justin Crawford (West Virginia) 6-0 202 4.55

*Jordan Scarlett (Florida) 5-10 213 4.55

Nick Wilson (Arizona) 5-10 199 4.53

Nyheim Heins (N.C. State) 5-9 197 4.52

WIDE RECEIVERS

Position Grade: A-

First Round Talent: Calvin Ridley, Courtland Sutton, Christian Kirk

*Calvin Ridley (Alabama) 6-1 188 4.48: For the second time in three years, the Alabama Crimson Tide may very well have the number 1 receiving prospect in the nation. Following in the footsteps of the Oakland Raiders' Amari Cooper, junior Calvin Ridley is ready for his early first-round moment. Possessing even better hands than Cooper, Ridley is an excellent route runner who knows how to find the open seam in the defense. Where Ridley comes up a bit short compared to Cooper is his wiry (code for thin) frame which could lead to issues against press cornerbacks. The speed is terrific though and that makes Ridley a threat to score whenever he finds open space with the football in his hands.

*Courtland Sutton (SMU) 6-4 216 4.51: Physically speaking, SMU's Courtland Sutton checks off almost all the boxes in terms of what a first-round wideout looks like. Sutton can use his 6-4 frame to ward off defenders and make the difficult catch. Also, good luck trying to deal with Sutton around the red zone where he could instantly catch double-digit scores as a rookie. While he does not have blazing speed, Sutton is capable of opening up on defenders when in the open field. Think a young Keyshawn Johnson here.

*Christian Kirk (Texas A & M) 5-11 200 4.43: Wow, look at that 40-time. Speed, speed, and more speed here from the explosive Christian Kirk who put up typically big numbers from the explosive Texas Tech offense. Kirk is a big play waiting to happen and he has drawn DeSean Jackson comparisons as a result. Like with Jackson, Kirk is going to have to deal with physical mismatches against bigger NFL corners and durability could be a challenge as well unless he adds weight.

James Washington (Oklahoma State) 6-1 205 4.50: The big-play deep threat in the Oklahoma State attack, James Washington complemented possession teammate Marcel Ateman in 2017. While Ateman was mostly a move-the-chains wideout, Washington supplied the bigger plays down the field with his quickness in and out of cuts and burner's speed. Had some concentration lapses that resulted in drops from time-to-time but generally, Washington did his job on a weekly basis. Somewhat a product of the spread system at Oklahoma State, Washington still has the athleticism and quickness off the snap to be a Day 2 pick.

Anthony Miller (Memphis) 5-11 190 4.52: Having served as Riley Ferguson's top target in the passing game, wideout Anthony Miller in the process put himself on the NFL Draft landscape. Taking full advantage of the pass-heavy offense, Miller caught 91 balls for 1,407 yards and 17 touchdowns in 2017; showcasing smooth route-running and big-play speed. Miller also possesses a good set of hands that can make the tough grab but he seriously needs to add some weight to deal with press coverage. Likely suited to a slot role in the NFL.

Marcel Ateman (Oklahoma State) 6-4 220 4.56: Red zone/possession receiver who will tower over many opposing DB's at the next level which alone ensures that Oklahoma State's Marcel Ateman will get a long look by some NFL team. Won't make many big plays down the field, as Ateman is a long-striding wideout who gets by as much on physicality, as he does with his plus jumping ability. Ateman also doesn't possess much explosion and will thus have to work off a deep-play threat on the other side.

*Arden Tate (Florida State) 6-5 225 4.56: Possession extraordinaire Arden Tate was held back with the season-ending injury to Seminoles QB Deondre Francois in the team's opener last September but the talent is evident. Yes, Tate is not going to make a high number of plays down the field given the fact he lacks the explosive speed out of his stance that some of the wideouts ranked above him possess but that doesn't mean he won't be a handful for defensive backs. Tate can get himself free from the jam given his height/strength and in the red zone, he will be a major force.

*Equanimeous St. Brown (Notre Dame) 6-4 205 4.50: Love this kid. While the offensive numbers with the Irish don't jump off the page, you can bet that Equanimeous Brown is a tremendous prospect who has a boatload of tools to offer his new organization. What becomes obvious when watching tape on Brown is that he is a tremendous route runner who sets up defenders well to make plays on the football. The hands grade out as good as any wideout in the draft as well; with Brown capable of making difficult catches in traffic. Adept at going up for jump balls, Brown could easily turn out to be the most productive wideout in the draft but with a cheaper price than Ridley and Sutton.

*Simmie Cobbs Jr. (Indiana) 6-4 220 4.55: Cobbs goes into the NFL Draft on a big high as he finished the 2017 season on a positive note, which included a big game against Urban Meyer's defense at Ohio State. Physically speaking, Cobbs Jr. has an excellent combination of size, strength, and speed and the so the upside is quite vast. Took a medical redshirt in 2016 and durability is a concern but Cobbs seems to have a knack for making plays. Another name to add to sleeper lists.

Jaleel Scott (New Mexico State) 6-6 215 4.57: While not a hotbed for NFL prospects, New Mexico State has an intriguing one in wideout Jaleel Scott. The reason Scott is drawing attention is due to his massive 6-6/215 frame which is insane height for the position. Right from the jump, Scott will be a one-on-one physical nightmare around the red zone and that alone will make him attractive. Of course, Scott has just average speed and won't make many big plays in between.

Parris Campbell (Ohio State) 6-1 208 4.44: The Buckeyes have had a knack for sending good wide receiver prospects to the NFL who have really panned out over the last ten years or so and Parris Campbell could be the next man up on that front. The deep-threat burner can take the top off any defense and you won't be catching Campbell if he gets a step on you. Unlike the similarly-skilled Christian Kirk, Campbell has decent enough size to prevent him from consistently being pushed off his routes. Dropped a few passes along the way and his lack of numbers at Ohio State could indicate some inconsistency.

Keke Coutee (Texas Tech) 5-11 180 4.53: You always have to take offensive numbers from the Air Raid offense of Texas Tech with a skeptical grain of salt and that goes for the output of wideout Keke Coutee. While the smooth route running and speed are easy to spot, Coutee has a very smallish frame that will ensure he will be a slot man only in the NFL. Can easily be pushed off his route and jammed effectively off the snap. Clear home run threat though if he can gain some separation.

Dante Pettis (Washington) 6-1 185 4.55: Ran too hot and cold for my liking. While Dante Pettis had his fair share of big games, there were also too many drops and stretches of completely being out of the flow of the offense. Checks out well when it comes to route running and making plays down the field but Pettis struggles when in tight and can't fight for the football in close due to his size limitations.

D.J. Chark (LSU) 6-3 187 4.53: Very interesting prospect in that LSU's D.J. Chark has impressive height but is a string bean weight-wise. As a result, Chark could be a nice red zone guy who can go up and catch the jump ball but consistency will be a challenge in the NFL given the fact he is incredibly skinny for his height.

*Deon Cain (Clemson) 6-2 200 4.51: Count this peanut stand as one that firmly believes Clemson's Deon Cain should stay in school for another year. He is mostly a one-trick pony in terms of being a deep threat wideout and he lacks fundamentals when one gazes at the tape. Drops have been a constant problem and Cain's numbers all took a dive last year compared to 2016 which is not the production plane a prospect wants to have going into the draft. Too rough around the edges at this point.

Cedric Wilson (Boise State) 6-3 188 4.59: Good catch radius here as Boise State's Cedric Wilson has impressive height and a good catch radius given his long arms/reach. There is a need to fill out some more as Wilson is very light in size/girth and that is important since he lacks the speed to make up for that deficiency.

*Deontay Burnett (USC) 6-0 170 4.47: Another receiving prospect who can contribute immediately on special teams and in the return game is the diminutive but lightning quick Deontay Burnett of USC. While clearly a physical mismatch against bigger NFL corners, Burnett can create open space in a hurry with his top-end speed and his route-running is above-average. Consistency will not be there given the size but Burnett's speed will ensure he gets a long look.

Darren Carrington (Utah) 6-2 195 4.52: Having transferred from Oregon to Utah prior to 2017, wideout Darren Carrington had a nice season in catching 70 passes for 980 yards and 6 scores. While nothing earth-shattering, Carrington seems to have some untapped potential which is worth a late-round stab. A possible late-bloomer considering Carrington didn't do much prior to last season, the measurables are just all right. Likely needs a season or learning before a meaningful contribution can be made.

*Antonio Callaway (Florida) 5-11 197 4.46: Big off-the-field trouble here as Callaway was suspended for the entire 2017 season due to being charged with a forgery felony. In addition to those serious charges, Callaway also has a noted drug problem that includes numerous failed tests. The real shame of it all is that Callaway has tremendous physical skills and the ability to be a top prospect without the trouble. Blessed with top-end speed, Callaway is a blazing talent who can open up yardage with little effort. Unfortunately, that talent takes a backseat to character issues and in today's NFL, Callaway is as radioactive as they get.

*Hunter Renfrow (Clemson) 5-10 180 4.54: Another of the Clemson playmakers on offense is slot man Hunter Renfrow who had some big catches during his collegiate career. The biggest, o course, was catching a touchdown pass in the 2016 championship game. While his lack of height holds Renfrow back some, he tends to take advantage of his speed in the slot to make big plays. Renfrow has always shown good hands and grabbing hold of a third receiver spot at the next level is entirely possible.

Michael Gallup (Colorado State) 6-1 200 4.56: Former junior college kid who was extremely productive once he reached Colorado State. Gallup hit the century mark in receptions in 2017 with an even 100 for 1,413 yards and 7 scores; showcasing top-notch fundamentals and route-running. Those skills helped Gallup overcome a lack of speed and explosion in-and-out of his cuts. Classic chain mover who won't make many highlight plays.

Jake Wieneke (South Dakota State) 6-4 215 4.58: When it comes to small-school prospects, almost always the intrigue centers on a physical characteristic such as the 6-4 height of South Dakota State's Jake Wieneke. That height allowed Wieneke to snag a ridiculous 16 touchdown receptions last season; an impressive number at any level. A man among boys at the lower leve of competition, Wieneke needs to develop his route running and ability to make catches in tight since he got by more on his athletic advantage at South Dakota State.

Allen Lazard (Iowa State) 6-5 222 4.60: Speaking of massive size, get a look at 6-6 Iowa Stat wideout Allen Lazard. That is freakish height Lazard will bring to his NFL team and instantly h will be a physical nightmare versus smaller professional corners. Unfortunately, Lazard is looking like a one-trick pony there as he is lacking speed and that deficiency makes him too slov in-and-out of his routes.

*Jauan Jennings (Tennessee) 6-3 205 4.55: In terms of Tennessee wideout Jauan Jennings, it is tough to give him a draft grade given the fact he missed virtually the whole 2017 season with dislocated wrist. He also dealt with some off-the-field trouble which adds to the red flags here. While you love the height and leaping ability, Jennings will be a no-go for many personnel exec this spring.

J'Mon Moore (Missouri) 6-3 205 4.54: Missouri's J'Mon Moore has a nice combination of siz and quickness, without being a burner. While he has a decent array of physical tools to work with, Moore also cut off routes too often and drops were an occasional problem. Finally, Moore doesn't have the leaping ability one would suspect given his height as he often lost one-on-one battles there and he could use some more weight.

D.J. Moore (Maryland) 5-11 215 4.56: Reminding many of former Maryland alum Stefon Diggs, D.J. Moore has the same slot-centric game that is predicated on smooth route-running ar good speed. While not a burner, Moore gets in and out of his cuts quickly and the hands grade out as above-average. Of course, the flip side is that Moore needs to stay almost exclusively in the slot due to a lack of height and strength. Can be easily pushed off his routes and knocked off stride.

Steve Ishmael (Syracuse) 6-2 209 4.54: You don't see many Syracuse offensive prospects since the Donovan McNabb era but wideout Steve Ishmael is on the radar after catching 105 passes as a senior in 2017. While eye-popping catch numbers in college don't always translate to the NFL level, the fact Ishmael has good height and good enough speed makes him worth a late-round stab.

Jester Weah (Pittsburgh) 6-3 210 4.52: While he is a big-play guy, Pittsburgh wideout Jester Weah is just an average prospect who may have to go the free agent route. Struggling to gain consistent separation due to a long-striding gait, Weah is mostly just a possession guy who doesn't wow you in any one area.

THE REST

Brandon Powell (Florida) 5-9 184 4.46

*Richie James (Middle Tennessee) 5-9 180 4.54

Austin Proehl (North Carolina) 5-10 175 4.54

TIGHT ENDS

Position Grade: C

First Round Talent: Mark Andrews

*Mark Andrews (Oklahoma) 6-5 250 4.78: The latest in what has been an impressive collection of early-round receiving talent at the tight end position will welcome in a new member this April in the form of Oklahoma's Mark Andrews. The junior was phenomenal offensively last season as he hauled in 58 balls for 906 yards and 8 scores in the pass-happy Sooner offense and in the process stamping him as a top draft prospect. At the very least, Andrews proved himself to be a terrific receiver who can contribute on that front right away. The problem is on the blocking side as Andrews is below-average there. Be that as it may, Andrews is also a big red zone threat who will be a threat catch 5-7 touchdowns as a rookie.

*Hayden Hurst (South Carolina) 6-5 250 4.65: While he won't be drafted nearly as high, South Carolina tight end Hayden Hurts has some similarities for 2016 first-round pick O.J. Howard. For one thing, Both Howard and Hurst were held back a bit by offenses that didn't throw often but both guys also have a terrific set of physical skills that could easily unlock their potential. What is interesting about Hurst is that he will be 25 once the 2018 NFL season gets underway due to his past as a pitcher in the Pittsburgh Pirates organization. With regards to his skill set, Hurst runs great routes and has the soft hands to consistently make plays in the passing game.

Mike Gesicki (Penn State) 6-6 252 4.74: Penn State tight end Mike Gesicki made good on his potential when he became a starter as a senior in 2017; hauling in 51 balls for 501 yards and 9 scores. Gesicki is a smooth route runner who finds the seam often enough down the middle of the field and around the red zone he is a tough cover. Blocking is just all right but Gesicki is decent enough there to not have to come out on obvious running plays. While not as gifted athletically as some of the higher-ranked tight ends, Gesicki looks like a solid future pro.

Dallas Goedert (South Dakota State) 6-4 260 4.73: Invited to the Senior Bowl on the strength of some video-game offensive numbers at small-school South Dakota State, tight end Dallas Goedert will have quite a few NFL execs checking him out leading up to the draft. Goedert seems to have all the requisite tools to become a very good receiving tight end at the next level as he combined textbook route running with a sure set of hands. Yes, he can't block your grandma but Goedert is a massive upside play who could be snagged in the middle rounds of the draft.

Troy Fumagalli (Wisconsin) 6-6 248 4.67: Despite an injury-plagued senior year, Wisconsin tight end Troy Fumagalli is quickly moving up the draft charts due to his tremendous physical tools and pass-receiving ability. While not a horrendous blocker, Fumagalli grades out very well on the receiving side of things. Showing impressive route running fundamentals, Fumagalli also is quite sure-handed. Not to be overlooked is the fact Fumagalli operated in a pro-style offense with the Badgers which will speed up the learning curve.

*Dalton Schultz (Stanford) 6-6 240 4.80: Along with Notre Dame and Miami, Stanford has a good track record of sending tight ends to the NFL. Like with previous alum Zach Ertz, Schultz is adept both in blocking and pass-receiving. Very strong and possessing a nasty demeanor, Schultz helped open up holes for running back Bryce Love throughout the season in 2017. While not featured much in the passing game, Schultz caught almost everything thrown his way. The fact Schultz didn't have gaudy offensive numbers at Stanford could cause his draft stock to slip some and on that front, he would become a potentially good sleeper.

Durham Smythe (Notre Dame) 6-4 245 4.73: "Tight End U" has another NFL prospect to offer the league in the form of senior Durham Smythe. Having dealt with numerous injuries during his collegiate career, the numbers are just not there from an offensive standpoint though. In Smythe's defense, however, he has some decent receiving ability and was often underutilized in the run-heavy ND offense. The success of the Notre Dame program when it comes to churning out tight ends will ensure Smythe will get a look somewhere and he may surprise.

Tyler Conklin (Central Michigan) 6-4 240 4.77: While a plodding runner, Central Michigan tight end Tyler Conklin is a junkyard dog type of player who caught the football well enough to put himself on the late-round radar for the 2018 NFL Draft. Conklin often did his best work in the red zone where he caught a high amount of touchdown passes.

Adam Breneman (UMASS) 6-5 255 4.76: Another small school tight end prospect who offers up impressive receiving numbers. Breneman sets up defenders well with nice route running and he almost always made the catch when the football was within his general radius. Wasn't asked to block much at UMASS and that was probably a good thing since Breneman struggled noticeably on that front. Like the upside here at least from a receiving standpoint.

*Caleb Wilson (UCLA) 6-5 235 4.69: Check out the rare speed here when it comes to the tight end position and then look at how much of a smooth receiver UCLA's Caleb Wilson was before he went down with a foot injury last season. Wilson has uncanny quickness and acceleration for a tight end prospect and he was a safety outlet for QB Josh Rosen for much of 2017. A bit on the finesse side given the light weight, Wilson will garner a lot of attention for what he can do both catching the football and running after the catch.

Chris Herndon (Miami Fla.) 6-4 252 4.73: Following in the footsteps of former teammate and current Cleveland Brown David Njoku, tight end Chris Herndon put forth some nice numbers in 2017 when he hauled in 40 balls for 477 yards and 4 scores. There is nothing flashy here when it comes to Herndon's game but he has enough both in the receiving and blocking side of things to at least catch on as a backup in the NFL.

Ian Thomas (Indiana) 6-5 248 4.73: Yes Indiana is far from a hotbed of NFL talent but tight end Ian Thomas is on the NFL radar after showcasing a solid receiving game in 2017. Thomas possesses a nice combination of size and speed but needs to refine his route running and ability to make plays in tight so he can maximize his potential.

DeAndre Goolsby (Florida) 6-4 240 4.70: Likely having to go the free agent route, Florida's DeAndre Goolsby was a big letdown for the Gators during his collegiate career. For one thing,

Goolsby struggled as a receiver; often dropping balls and showcasing choppy footwork. Injuries also were a constant issue as well.

*C.J. Conrad (Kentucky) 6-5 245 4.70: Kentucky's C.J. Conrad is a bit of a unicorn at the tight end position due to his lack of bulk/strength but at the same time possessing some receiving upside. A foot injury that eventually led to surgery took out half of Conrad's junior season but he showed enough offensively to get a free agent invite somewhere.

Cam Serigne (Wake Forest) 6-3 250 4.72: What is interesting about the collegiate career of Wake Forest tight end Cam Serigne is that his offensive numbers dipped every year from a 54-catch freshman campaign. While Serigne knows how to catch the football and get open, he was a terrible blocker who also often cut off his routes too early.

Marcus Baugh (Ohio State) 6-5 258 4.79: A solid blocker who also can catch the odd pass, Ohio State tight end Marcus Baugh could snag a seventh-round pick if he is lucky. Urban Meyer praised Baugh's ability to catch the football but the fact of the matter is that he was not utilized much there to make him more than a speculative pick.

THE REST

Jake Roh (Boise State) 6-3 227 4.72

Jeb Blazevich (Georgia) 6-5 248 4.75

Brandon Lingen (Minnesota) 6-5 250 4.76

Ethan Wolf (Tennessee) 6-6 258 4.74

Ryan Yurachek (Marshall) 6-3 232 4.71

OFFENSIVE TACKLE

Position Grade: A-

First Round Talent Mike McGlinchey, Kolton Miller, Orlando Brown, Connor Williams

Mike McGlinchey (Notre Dame) 6-7 310 5.30: Other then maybe Kolton Miller, Notre Dame's Mike McGlinchey is the top left tackle prospect in the 2018 NFL Draft. With Notre Dame already having a very good reputation developing high-end NFL blockers, McGlinchey should be a high first-round pick given his excellent blend of size and athleticism. Having been a starter since his sophomore season, McGlinchey has a ton of experience under his belt and you can see that in his textbook stance and ability to set up quickly off the snap. Love the footwork here as McGlinchey engages his opponent with terrific hand placement and has the skills to open solid holes in the run game. While his run blocking grades out better than his pass protection, McGlinchey is still very solid at the latter. Looks like a sure Pro Bowler real soon.

*Kolton Miller (UCLA): 6-8 310 5.20: While a bit raw, UCLA's Kolton Miller showcased some dominant run blocking as a collegiate and in tight was a handful for opposing defenders in pass protection. The one clear issue here is that Miller tends to struggle versus speed rushers and that could necessitate a move to the right side. There is nice upside here however and Miller has all the ingredients needed to be a high-end player.

Conor Williams (Texas) 6-6 290 5.10: A knee injury took out a big chunk of Texas offensive tackle Conor Williams' junior season but prior to that, he was considered one of the better prospects at his position for the 2018 NFL Draft. What is clear is that despite carrying some nice upside, Williams is a bit of a work in progress as he is very slight in size for a tackle and there is an obvious lack of power here as well. Williams' footwork needs to be ironed out as well as he too often yielded pressure from more powerful defensive ends. If Williams does fill out a bit and get coached up, he can develop into a solid right tackle.

Orlando Brown (Oklahoma) 6-8 360 5.45: Just massive size here both in height and weight. Once Brown gets his grip on a defender, he can completely blow him out of the play and open gaping holes in the run game. Brown excels at run blocking but gets a bit exposed when having to deal with speedy edge rushers. Given the mammoth size he carries, Brown is a bit slow off the snap and that gets him into trouble yielding ground to quicker defensive ends. As a result, Brown is more suited to being a right tackle or even possibly moving inside.

Chukwuma Okorafor (Western Michigan) 6-6 330 5.19: Finesse blocker who combined textbook technique and the hand placement to open up consistent holes in the run game. The fact Okorafor struggled somewhat in pass protection at a smaller school is concerning however and he likely will have to stay exclusively on the right side given that not-so-small issue. Be that as it may, Okorafor has the very impressive strength to push defenders around with ease. If he can get his timing down better when dealing with speedy edge rusher, Okorafor could turn out to be a good investment.

Isaiah Wynn (Georgia) 6-2 302 5.10: When you help make not one but two running backs on your own team become high-end NFL draft picks, prospect hounds take a bit more interest in those who do the blocking. As part of the massive run-based attack that spearheaded the Georgi Bulldogs to the National Championship game, left tackle Isaiah Wynn more than placed himself on the draft landscape with his refined run blocking and powerful low-center of gravity. On the physical side of things, Wynn is a bit small for an outside blocker but he has the quickness off the snap and good knee-bend to hold anchor. Wynn also has some snarl to his game as well which his NFL coach will love.

Dalton Risner (Kansas State) 6-5 300 5.22: Redshirt junior Kansas State tackle Dalton Risner has really risen up the draft charts over the last year as he put forth a very nice 2017 campaign. Having also played well previously at center, Risner dominated at times last season at right tackle for K-State. Risner has very potent brute strength to control his defender and at times completely push him out of the play. He also plays with good knee bend and holds anchor well. At times Risner does let a speed rusher gain the edge and his run blocking is not at the standard of his pass protection. Overall though, you are looking at a very good right tackle prospect.

Tyrell Crosby (Oregon) 6-5 310 5.28: Possessing a terrific frame for the left tackle position, the ceiling goes pretty high for Oregon's Tyrell Crosby. The issue here is that Crosby lacks experience as he missed almost all of 2016 with a foot injury but he graded out very well in his senior campaign. Crosby was directly responsible for quite a bit of the success of running back Royce Freeman; opening up sizable holes consistently in the run game. While the latter is Crosby's strength, he held up pretty well in pass protection (while not being dominant by any means). Overall, Crosby can stick on the left side given what we have seen from him in 2017.

*Brian O'Neill (Pittsburgh) 6-6 305 5.10: Boy has Pittsburgh's Brian O'Neill run the gamut of positions going back to high school. Originally a wideout at the latter level, O'Neill made his way to Pittsburgh as a tight end but soon moved to the offensive line where he has experience both at right and left tackle. What stands out here is the speed which can be attributed to his pas as a receiver and this helps O'Neill fly off the snap and quickly get into the play. While not the strongest player in the world, O'Neill holds anchor well enough but needs to be careful not to play too high which was sometimes an issue.

Martinas Rankin (Mississippi State) 6-5 307 5.20: Having gone through some clear ups and downs in his collegiate career from a performance perspective, the NFL outlook on Mississippi State tackle Martinis Rankin is a bit muddled. On the positive side, Rankin had a very good 2016 where he showed nice pass protection skills and graded out well in the run game. 2017 wa not as impressive on those fronts however and so that is why there is a great deal of uncertainty here. At the very least, Rankin possesses fluid movement and the toughness to scrap in tight with defenders. Where he gets into trouble is against speed rushers where his lack of refined technique in pass blocking sometimes gets taken advantage of. This one could go either way.

*Andre Dillard (Washington State) 6-5 300 5.14: You're looking at one of the more athletic left tackle prospects in the entire 2018 NFL Draft when it comes to Washington State's Andre Dillard. Possessing uncanny quickness and short-burst speed for an offensive lineman, Dillard can keep plays alive down the field with those skills. He really opened eyes as a junior in 2017 under this approach and Dillard anchored himself adequately against bigger defensive lineman as well. While Dillard does need to add a bit more weight, he is moving up draft boards fast this winter.

Desmond Harrison (West Georgia) 6-7 300 5.10: Former Texas Longhorn recruit Desmond Harrison was booted out of school due to a series of failed drug tests and so right off the bat the guy is a character concern. Harrison did rebound at West Georgia where he kept himself clean and showed intriguing athleticism at left tackle. While you have to consider the level of competition when evaluating Harrison, what becomes easy to identify is how he possesses crucial left tackle tools such as size and quickness off the snap to be an impact player. The off-the-field concerns are a big red flag however and Harrison will slip quite a bit because of that trouble.

Brandon Parker (North Carolina A @ T) 6-8 310 5.20: Having absolutely dominated at the FCS level, North Carolina A @ T's Brandon Parker got a much-deserved invite to the Senior Bowl where he could really boost his stock. Parker was a dominant pass protector while in college, showcasing excellent footwork and agility; while also using brute force when needed in order to thwart defenders. Where he did struggle a bit was in run blocking and that has to be his focus in order to make it in the NFL.

Austin Corbett (Nevada) 6-4 305 5.12: Since he was installed as a starting lineman for Nevada as a freshman, tackle Austin Corbett has a ridiculous amount of collegiate experience to fall back on as he heads into the NFL Draft. Corbett has played extensively both at left and right tackle and receiving a Senior Bowl invite was another feather in his draft cap. In terms of his game, Corbett gets up into his stance quickly off the snap and plays with a mean streak. Corbett does his best work in the run-blocking game; firing off into defenders will good hand placement and technique. His lateral quickness is not terrific though and he yields pressure against speedier edge rushers.

Jamarco Jones (Ohio State) 6-5 310 5.20: If there was a way for Ohio State tackle Jamarco Jones to return as a super senior, he would need to do it since his 2017 campaign was a mess. Jones struggled badly at times when it came to pass blocking, with his utter lack of speed/athleticism standing out there. While Jones plays with snarl and gets a push in the run game, he will need to get schooled out of his ugly 2017 habits to contribute to his NFL squad.

Alex Cappa (Humboldt State) 6-7 305 5.14: While he will face quite a steep NFL learning curve coming from a D-II program, Humboldt State offensive tackle Alex Cappa absolutely lit up the competition at this level by earning the GNAC Offensive Lineman of the Year award four straight years. That alone will raise the interest meter around personnel execs and so will Cappa's 6-7 size and solid frame. Of course, Cappa rarely had to deal with the type of speed rushers he will soon encounter and that could change the narrative quickly in a negative sense. While he could easily be a miss, Cappa could also be a true diamond in the rough find.

*Nick Gates (Nebraska) 6-6 295 5.18: Thought it would be a good idea that Nebraska left tackle Nick Gates returned to school for his senior year in order to put on some more weight and refine his pass blocking a bit but the kid declared for the draft last December. There were some injury troubles during his career with the Cornhuskers and Gates struggled in pass protection too often to think of him as anything but a late-round project.

Ike Boettger (Iowa) 6-6 307 5.08: By the time you read this, Iowa tackle Ike Boettger will either be going into the NFL Draft or will be granted an injury redshirt to return to the Hawkeyes in 2018. The redshirt would be due to the fact Boettger missed almost his entire 2017 season with a torn Achilles tendon and that injury dulled any sort of draft momentum he might have had. A former tight end, Boettger was a decent right tackle but his ceiling was limited due to mediocre strength that made him a bit of a blocking liability versus more powerful ends.

THE REST

Bentley Spain (North Carolina) 6-6 300 5.09

Timon Parris (Stony Brook) 6-5 310 5.10
David Bright (Stanford) 6-5 293 5.32

Cole Madison (Washington State) 6-5 314 5.24

Martez Ivy (Florida) 6-5 305 5.15

Casey Tucker (Stanford) 6-6 300 5.32

K.C. McDermott (Miami Fla.) 6-6 310 5.29

Brendan Mahon (Penn State) 6-4 315 5.28

OFFENSIVE GUARD

Position Grade: C+

First Round Talent: Quenton Nelson

Quenton Nelson (Notre Dame) 6-5 325 5.15: If he were a tackle instead of a guard, Notre Dame's Quenton Nelson would be a locked-in top ten pick overall in the 2018 NFL Draft. Be that as it may, Nelson is so talented that he may actually come close to reaching that tier. This speaks to how dominant a blocker Nelson was in his collegiate career and he easily can follow in the Pro Bowl footsteps of former Irish guard Zach Martin. Nelson is a classic road-grading blocker in the run game; using his massive power to open up gaping holes along the line. As great as he is in the run game, Nelson also has very impressive fluidity and lateral agility for a big man and his pass protection grades out well above-average. There are very few holes to speak of here and Nelson is set to be a perennial high-end player for the lucky team that drafts him.

Will Hernandez (UTEP) 6-3 330 5.25: Possessing the classic wide-body required of being a guard, UTEP's Will Hernandez is in the running to be the next player selected from the position behind consensus number 1 Quenton Nelson. While Hernandez is a bit on the short side, he plays with excellent knee bend and generates quite a bit of push off the snap due to his top-notch strength. Lauded as a workout warrior, Hernandez is a big plus in the run blocking game and is no slouch in pass protection either.

Braden Smith (Auburn) 6-6 303 5.10: This guy belongs in a muscle magazine. Wow is Auburn guard Braden Smith a physical marvel as his feats in the weight room are legendary and his squat/bench/vertical numbers are all off the charts. There is some serious athleticism and power to work with here and that more than makes up for the fact Smith is very light for a guard. Capable of winning battles in tight versus bigger defensive linemen, Smith only has to work on avoiding playing too high in his stance which can get him pushed back quickly against pro players.

Maea Teuhema (Southeastern Louisiana) 6-5 315 5.29: Be sure not to let the small school fool you when it comes to the ability of Southeastern Louisiana guard Maea Teuhema as he was originally a member of the LSU Tigers before he got booted out of school due to chronic academic issues. While the bombing out of LSU due to poor grades could be a red flag in terms of learning/digesting an NFL playbook, Teuhema has the raw power and decent enough athleticism to be a solid prospect. Having experience as a left tackle is a plus but Teuhema is slated for the inside at the NFL level due to below-average quickness off the snap.

*Scott Quessenberry (UCLA) 6-4 314 5.29: There are NFL bloodlines here as UCLA guard Scott Quessenberry is the brother of Houston Texans offensive lineman David. As far as Scott is concerned, he is coming out early after playing well in a high-profile spot protecting QB Josh Rosen. While Quessenberry is a bit on the small side for a prospective NFL guard, he showed impressive smarts and a refined blocking technique to cement him on the radar of league executives. There are issues here, however; primarily of which is Quessenberry's shaky run blocking. While he has generally held up well in pass protection due to putting forth a low center of gravity to help maintain leverage, Quessenberry was not always successful when trying to open up holes in the run game. His lack of above-average power is the reason for this as Quessenberry struggled in tight against the bigger defensive linemen.

Sean Welsh (Iowa) 6-3 295 5.08: Having come off a disappointing senior year, perhaps the best thing you can say about the draft prospects of Iowa offensive lineman Sean Welsh is that he literally had experience at every position there while in school. Clearly, Welsh has the athleticism and smarts to handle all of those varying responsibilities but his pass protection was very shaky at times last season. In addition, Welsh really needs to add some weight or he will be pushed around by defensive lineman on a weekly basis as a pro.

Wyatt Teller (Virginia Tech) 6-5 315 5.29: Solid but unspectacular is how you would describe Virginia Tech guard Wyatt Teller. That is because Teller doesn't do any one thing great but at the same time, he is fundamentally sound in most areas. While Teller does have decent size, he doesn't move all that well in space which makes him somewhat shaky in pass protection. He does take up quite a bit of ground along the line though and Teller gets a good push in the run game by playing with leverage through a low stance with decent knee bend.

*Taylor Hearn (Clemson) 6-5 330 5.22: After being named all-conference in the ACC in 2017 for the perennially contending Clemson Tigers, guard Taylor Hearn declared early for the NFL Draft. While he could have boosted his stock by returning for his senior season, Hearn will lean on his good power and size to open up holes in the run game which was a big weapon for Clemson during his tenure there. The problem is that Hearn is nothing special as a pass protector and that is not a label you want to carry into the NFL where that side of the offensive attack has never been more prominent.

*Sam Jones (Arizona State) 6-5 290 5.09: USC guard Sam Jones comes out early with the hope his impressive speed and athleticism for an offensive lineman will catch the attention of the draft community. While those are nice attributes to possess, Jones also lacks a clear position as he is less than 300 pounds and struggles in tight against stronger defensive linemen. Yes, Jones has experience at every position along the line but that also can be a negative when it comes to figuring out where to place him going forward.

Larry Allen (Harvard) 6-4 285 5.00: Yes Larry Allen from Harvard is the son of Larry Allen the perennial All-Pro offensive guard for the Dallas Cowboys who is on the short list as one of the greatest to ever play the position. What is interesting is that Allen the son failed to inherit his father's freakish strength and his lack of size is a major impediment to him being drafted. While the name will be a story during the draft, it looks like Allen Jr. is nothing but a seventh-round pick at best.

THE REST

Wilson Bell (Auburn) 6-6 334 5.19

Brandon Fanaika (Stanford) 6-3 321 5.35

Tyrone Crowder (Clemson) 6-2 340 5.19

Viane Talamaivao (USC) 6-2 315 5.31

Cody O'Connell (Washington State) 6-9 354 5.19

CENTERS

Position Grade: D+

First Round Talent: None

Billy Price (Ohio State) 6-4 315 5.34: One of the stronger players at any position in the 2018 NFL Draft undoubtedly is Ohio State center Billy Price. Price has the pure brute strength to handle bigger defensive tackles; playing with a low-center of gravity and leg drive. A true road-grading run blocker, Price was a running back's best friend. The problem here centers on Price's overly grabby approach when it comes to pass protection and he has the high penalty totals to prove it. Having surrendered more pressure than you would like, Price is not a finished product just yet.

Bradley Bozeman (Alabama) 6-5 319 5.25: A firm anchor in the middle of the Alabama Crimson Tide offensive line the last few seasons has been center Bradley Bozeman. Durable and smart, Bozeman controls the interior of the line nicely with textbook technique. Bozeman can fire off the snap quickly and he has the brute strength to get immediate push. He struggles at times with faster interior lineman who can slip gaps but overall Bozeman should make it as a Day 2 selection.

Frank Ragnow (Arkansas) 6-5 317 5.24: While the center position is arguably one of the worst when it comes to NFL talent for the 2018 Draft, the Arkansas Razorbacks' Frank Ragnow is on the short list of being the top prospect among the group along with Ohio State's Billy Price. Unfortunately for Ragnow, his senior season was cut short due to a serious ankle injury that required surgery. While that was a rough way to end his collegiate career, Ragnow previously showed high-end ability while giving up almost zero pressure on the QB from the middle. Blessed with good size and athletic ability for a big man, Ragnow holds anchor very well and keeps his hands moving at all times to keep defenders from gaining leverage. Having experience as a guard is also a plus. If the injury was taken out of the equation, Ragnow had a chance for being a second-round pick.

Austin Golson (Auburn) 6-5 304 5.22: Having played all over the line during his career at Auburn, Austin Golson did his best work in the middle calling the protections. While Golson does bear responsibility for an overall poor year by the Auburn line in 2017, he generally graded out well enough both in pass protection and run blocking. Golson can move a little in helping to keep the play going down the field, bull rushing D-tackles are a struggle for him.

Coleman Shelton (Washington) 6-4 293 5.10: With a very slight frame for an offensive lineman but impressive speed, Washington's Coleman Shelton is best suited for the center position. Lauded for leadership and high character by the Washington staff, Shelton is a good late-round prospect who can possibly latch on as a backup lineman.

Brian Allen (Michigan State) 6-1 304 5.12: It is going to be tough for Michigan State center Brian Allen to make it as a pro given his lack of strength needed to handle nose tackles and also for his short height. You just don't see any offensive linemen in the pros with that combination of size/strength and so Allen is likely going to have to catch on as a free agent.

Mason Cole (Michigan) 6-5 305 5.09: Another line prospect who has played every position there during his college career, Michigan's Mason Cole looks like just an average prospect who will likely be a Day 3 choice. The problem here is that Cole is a shaky pass protector due to clear strength shortcomings and his run blocking ran too hold-and-cold as well. Likely slated for backup duty as a pro.

THE REST

Tony Adams (N.C. State) 6-2 300 5.22:

Sam Mustipher (Notre Dame) 6-2 305 5.24:

Nick Linder (Miami Fla.) 6-3 302 5.22

DEFENSIVE END

Position Grade: B

First Round Talent: Bradley Chubb, Marcus Davenport, Arden Key, Klelin Ferrell

Bradley Chubb (N.C. State) 6-4 275 4.80: When it comes to pass rushing defensive maestro Bradley Chubb of N.C. State, you are looking at one of the top players in the entire 2018 NFL Draft. When you draw up what a pro pass rusher would look like, Chubb is certainly it as he combines excellent speed/burst off the snap with impressive strength. Having collected 20.5 sacks the last two seasons combined, Chubb knows how to get up the field in a hurry to wreak havoc. What really does put Chubb into the prospect stratosphere is the fact that he can generate a rush both with his speed around the edge but also in fighting himself free from in close. As an added bonus, Chubb's long arms knock down a high number of passes as well.   Since he also grades out nicely in stopping the run, Chubb looks like a possible Michael Strahan-like pro which certainly speaks to the massive upside.

Marcus Davenport (UTSA) 6-7 256 4.77: It took awhile but UTSA's Marcus Davenport has fully blossomed into a top-tier NFL defensive end prospect that should have him going behind only Bradley Chubb in Round 1 this April. Davenport's 6-7 height doesn't seem to inhibit his speed off the edge and that is a physical combination that NFL executives drool over. That height also allows Davenport to bust up plenty of running plays and also to knock down a high number of throws. When all the physical talent like Davenport comes together as one like it did for him in 2017, a major move up the draft board ensues as we are seeing here now.

*Dorance Armstrong Jr. (Kansas) 6-4 241 4.60: Serving as a true diamond in the muck that was the Kansas Jayhawks football program, speedy defensive end Dorance Armstrong Jr. is really catching the eye of NFL draftniks around the league. It is obvious looking at the 40-time that Armstrong Jr. has the type of explosive speed that makes for a highly impactful pass rusher but that ability lies a bit dormant given the fact he was constantly being double-teamed while with Kansas. There is a bit of the unknown with Armstrong Jr. as a result of how bad the Jayhawks were but boy that speed can really do some damage. For all the speed Armstrong Jr. brings to the table, however, the fact of the matter is that he will likely struggle to shed blocks unless he puts on more weight. Operating at 241 pounds in the NFL will be very difficult for Armstrong Jr. to get past hulking offensive linemen and so that is a not-so-small issue that makes him a bit of a risky pick.

*Arden Key (LSU) 6-5 260 4.70: Wow was it a rough season for LSU defensive end prospect Arden Key. Widely considered one of the potential top picks for the 2018 NFL draft prior to the 2017 collegiate season, Key endured what could only be described as one big year of frustration. The problems started when Key underwent shoulder surgery last spring and then degenerated into his weight ballooning when the season kicked off. Add in a slew of additional injuries that had Key's playing status in flux most of the season and one can see why 2017 was so troubling. Clearly Key did not go out with a bang and his draft stock is now all over the map based on his underwhelming season with the Tigers. The first concern, of course, centers on Key's penchant for getting hurt and also his conditioning. Having blown up to 270 pounds (after previously playing at 240), Key has to answer some maturity question marks with regards to taking care of himself. On the positive side, Key really flashes some big-time pass rushing ability that centers on his explosion and breakneck speed off the snap. Lauded as the better pure athlete when in top shape than Bradley Chubb, it really comes down to whether or not Key can stay on the field and take care of himself.

*Klelin Ferrell (Clemson) 6-5 265 4.77: Given the injury issues surrounding LSU's Arden Key, the mantle of number 3 defensive end in the 2018 NFL Draft (behind N.C. State's Bradley Chubb and USTA's Marcus Davenport) will likely fall to Clemson junior Klelin Ferrell. The Clemson defense has been lauded for their dominant units the last three seasons and a lot of that was achieved through the pass rushing prowess of Ferrell who served as a constant headache for offensive tackles coming off the edge. Yes, Ferrell plays a bit off fellow Clemson end Austin Bryant (and vice versa) but there is no denying the sheer speed and instant acceleration he has off the snap. Ferrell is adept at quickly getting to the edge and closing ground with his tremendous short-area burst to get to the quarterback. Sometimes Ferrell is guilty of over-running the play (giving up big rushing gains as a result) but the effort is always there. You would like to see someone with Ferrell's height get his hands on the ball more (just one pass batted last season) but this is a clear first-round pick by any measurement.

Justin Lawler (Southern Methodist) 6-4 265 4.72: Want to know who has the highest pass rushing grade in the entire 2018 NFL Draft according to Pro Football Focus? Try under-the-radar Southern Methodist defensive end Justin Lawler who picked up six sacks and an insane 31 QB pressures despite constant double-teams in 2017. While there is no denying the fact Lawler benefited from playing at a smaller school with regards to padding his resume, the measurables all scream out high-end pick as he combined terrific burst off the edge with the hand skills to fight off blockers in tight.

*Austin Bryant (Clemson) 6-4 265 4.77: The other half of the insane pass rushing duo at Clemson (along with Klelin Ferrell), Austin Bryant is putting himself close to first-round consideration just like his teammate. While he is not as strong as Ferrell, Bryant has just as much explosion off the snap and that helped him collect 7.5 sacks last season. Bryant anticipates the snap well and uses good leverage to gain the edge at a high rate. Improving in stopping the run, Bryant seems to hint there is another level or two in his development.

Harold Landry (Boston College) 6-3 250 4.67: Pass-rushing dynamo Harold Landry of Boston College didn't have the ending he anticipated for the team in 2017 as he missed the last four games of the year with a severe ankle injury. Prior to that, however, Landry continued to showcase impressive pass rushing ability that led to a massive 21.5 sacks the last two seasons despite the missed time. Clearly, Landry knows how to disrupt the passing game and his pure speed/acceleration off the snap grades out very highly. What keeps Landry a notch below the top ends in the 2018 NFL Draft is the fact that he has been a liability against the run throughout his collegiate career Too often Landry overruns the play and his tackling is far from textbook as he resorts to grabbing instead of wrapping up. A pass rushing specialist is still a highly coveted commodity however and so Landry should be picked among the first two rounds of the draft.

Duke Ejiofor (Wake Forest) 6-4 270 4.73: It was a somewhat disappointing year for pass rushing Wake Forest defensive end Duke Ejiofor as he went from picking up 10.5 sacks as a junior to netting just 6.5 in 2017. While Ejiofor still was a force on that side of the ball, his draft stock took a bit of a hit for the dip in numbers. Be that as it may, Ejiofor is a solid prospect who possesses long arms, a strong base, and enough pure speed to generate consistent pressure. There were some dry spells where it seemed Ejiofor failed to be an impact player but there are evident tools to work with here. The question is that the ceiling may not go much higher then what we already are seeing.

*Sam Hubbard (Ohio State) 6-5 266 4.78: Ohio State defensive end Sam Hubbard certainly went out with a bang as he completely wrecked the USC passing game in the Cotton Bowl by registering 2.5 sacks and 3.5 TFL's. While Hubbard's collegiate sack totals did not exactly jump off the page, he got better the more 2017 went on which is the kind of developmental plane NFL execs are searching for. Hubbard relies on his power and drive much more than pure speed to generate heat on the QB but it works just fine for him. What is also impressive physically is that Hubbard uses his long arms to serve as an asset in stopping the run; while also getting his hands on a decent amount of passes. A very hard-working kid who gets the most out of his ability.

Chad Thomas (Miami Fla.) 6-6 265 4.78: Miami Florida defensive end Chad Thomas is another one of those hot-and-cold players who keep personnel executives up at night. While he does showcase very solid run-stopping ability, Thomas also needs to improve on his pass rushing game which right now is very ordinary. Racking up just 3.5 sacks as a senior bear out this concern but the athleticism is also hinting that more ability there could be on the way.

*Olasunkanmi Adeniyi (Toledo) 6-2 251 4.68: One of the more unheralded defensive ends in college football last season was Toledo pass-rushing maven Olasunkanmi Adeniyi. Both his game and his name were a load for opposing players as Adeniyi relied on big-time quickness off the edge to rack up 8.5 sacks and 19.5 TFL's last season. Of course, it becomes a bit of a different discussion when the topic shifts to Adeniyi's NFL prospects given the fact he is very short for a defensive lineman at 6-2 and he is almost solely reliant on speed to get into the backfield. What should really help Adeniyi, however, is the fact he is an excellent run stopper. Using textbook tackling fundamentals, Adeniyi's is not strictly a one-dimensional player which will only help him in the draft.

Marcell Frazier (Missouri) 6-5 260 4.74: Another example of a workmanlike edge rusher who gains most of his numbers through sheer effort is Missouri defensive end Marcell Frazier. When dissecting Frazier's game, what quickly jumps out is his 6-5 height and very long arms that make him one of the best in the draft at swatting away passes. Frazier also is a very good run stopper who uses those long arms to eat up space. On the pass rushing side of things, Frazier tends to run hot-and-cold there given his lack of pure acceleration off the snap. Frazier often gets into the backfield through winning one-on-one battles as opposed to quickly gaining the edge.

Breeland Speaks (Ole Miss) 6-3 285 4.79: More of a 4-3 end at the next level, Ole Miss's Breeland Speaks is an overall solid prospect but with a limited amount of upside. Speaks has picked up 14 sacks the last two seasons, so there are some pass rush chops here but Speaks gets by mostly on strength and the ability to fight up the field. We really like how Speaks holds anchor well and that also allows him to pick up a decent amount of tackles in the run game.

*Josh Sweat (Florida State) 6-5 250 4.75: While not a finished product, Florida State defensive end Josh Sweat has all the tools and makeup to be a very intriguing sleeper. Capable of playing both end and outside linebacker, Sweat hints at some impressive pass rushing ability due to his speed off the edge. The raw mechanics are lacking here however and that is why Sweat was quite inconsistent in 2017. Injuries have undermined Sweat while at Florida State and that has helped keep the raw numbers down as well. A history of knee trouble no doubt is a red flag but Sweat has the type of untapped potential that could have him shooting up the draft board as April approaches.

Ade Aruna (Tulane) 6-4 265 4.70: Along the same lines as Josh Sweat, Tulane's Ade Aruna is quickly gaining a following in the draft community due to his impressive speed and agility for a defensive end. Aruna was just getting by on pure athletic ability while in college as he only began playing football late in high school. The fact Aruna is very raw but yet still was productive will make him a popular sleeper in the middle rounds of the draft. The lack of experience does show in tape in terms of Aruna overrunning plays and hesitating in space which allows some big plays in the run game.

Tyquan Lewis (Ohio State) 6-4 260 4.74: With 22 sacks over the last three seasons, Ohio State defensive end Tyquan Lewis has the numbers to gain some draft interest. However, there are questions about how much of those numbers Lewis earned with regards to benefiting from Sam Hubbard being on the other side of the defensive line. The athletic numbers are just ordinary here and Lewis doesn't excel at any one thing. Still, Lewis finds his way to the football at a high clip and so he will be a somewhat boring but decent mid-round pick.

*Jaylen Ferguson (Louisiana Tech) 6-5 255 4.72: By the time you read this, Louisiana Tech defensive end Jaylen Ferguson may have decided to go back to school. On the fence whether to declare for the NFL Draft as of this writing, it is our opinion that a move back to school would be the best course of action since Ferguson had a somewhat disappointing junior year. After racking up 14.5 sacks in 2016, Ferguson dropped back to a still impressive 6 last season. The dip was likely due to Ferguson drawing more double-teams but it was concerning that he was not able to consistently fight his way free from in tight. That might suggest Ferguson is simply a one-dimensional speed rusher and his smaller school background means that some of his pass rushing numbers need to be taken with a bit of a grain of salt.

Ja'Von Roland-Jones (Arkansas State) 6-2 244 4.75: Having won the Sun Belt Player of the Year Award, Arkansas State defensive end Ja'Von Rolland-Jones is being lauded as the top defensive prospect from the "Group Of Five." One can see physically why Rolland-Jones had to settle for Arkansas State as both his height and weight are below-average for an NFL defensive end prospect. Due to the lack of size/strength, Rolland-Jones will likely have to serve as an outside linebacker at the NFL level since he won't be able to fight free from offensive tackles right off the snap. Despite that shortcoming, Rolland-Jones knows his way to the football as he racked up 13.5 sacks in 2017 and also was a constant presence in disrupting the running game.

Kyle Fitts (Utah) 6-4 265 4.84: It is virtually impossible to give an adequate appraisal of Utah defensive end Kyle Fitts in relation to a draft grade considering he has barely played the last two years due to some incredibly poor injury luck. You have to go all the way back to 2015 when Fitts opened some eyes by picking up 7 sacks to see the potential that lies here. The long arms that Fitts possesses helped him also knock down a high number of passes but again the fact he has barely played the last two seasons make him a true wild card.

Marquis Haynes (Ole Miss) 6-3 222 4.64: Very experienced Ole Miss defensive end Marquis Haynes was an underrated/productive player for the team during his collegiate career; having tied the all-time SEC sacks mark with former Tennessee star Derek Barnett. While Haynes knows how to get to the QB, his NFL outlook is a bit murkier given his short and very light frame. A move to outside linebacker in a 4-3 alignment is likely needed once Haynes gets drafted due to his lack of strength in tight but the motor always runs high here. Haynes will likely work best as a situational pass rusher at the NFL level given the size limitations but there is some ability here.

*Hercules Mata'afa (Washington State) 6-2 255 4.90: Washington State defensive tackle Hercules Mata'afa will first have to move out from the middle and to defensive end or outside linebacker once he gets drafted into the NFL this April. This is due to the fact Mata'afa is very small to be a defensive tackle and so his hard-nosed pass rushing approach will work so much better on the outside. It is rushing the passer that Mata'afa does best as he was constantly disrupting opposing QB's during his collegiate career and this despite lacking in pure speed. Mata'afa uses excellent hand-to-hand skills to quickly shed blocks and fight his way up the field and this is how he generates most of his pressure. That skill will not be as potent in the NFL against bigger opposing lineman but Mata'afa should make his way as a situational rusher once drafted.

Jesse Aniebonam (Maryland) 6-3 259 4.77: Serving as a classic player without a set position due to a lack of a physical attribute, Maryland defensive end/OLB Jesse Aniebonam is likely going to have to make it as a free agent in order to play in the pros. The problem with Aniebonam is that he is too small for defensive end and too slow for outside linebackers and that makes his draft prospects quite iffy. Making matters worse, Aniebonam missed virtually all of 2017 with an injury.

Kemoko Turay (Rutgers) 6-5 252 4.77: While he has a nice combination of size and speed, Rutgers defensive end Kemoko Turay has been mostly all potential and little production the last three seasons. Things started off well as Turay was named to the All-Freshman All-America Team in 2014 in racking up 7 sacks but he has a grand total of 7 more the last three seasons. That is not a good indication of what Turay's NFL potential could be and so he is set for very late round consideration this spring.

Da'Shawn Hand (Alabama) 6-4 273 4.84: Even Nick Saban gets it wrong on some recruits and that certainly was the case when it came to defensive end Da'Shawn Hand. After coming out of high school as the number 1 recruit in the entire nation, Hand has been nothing but an unproductive enigma with the Crimson Tide. Showing little in the way of a pass rushing ability and barely making a dent in opposing team's backfields, Hand was a complete bust all the way around. Throw in poor speed and so-so strength and Hand will possibly not even get drafted.

Mike Love (South Florida) 6-4 260 4.67: This is one kid who has a chance to catch on as a seventh-round pick as South Florida's Mike Love is lauded for his unrelenting work ethic and never-ending motor. While the frame is slight in size, Love gets up the field with a nice burst and picks up heat from the edge through this mode of attack. He struggled in tight given the lack of strength and Love will be prone to being completely pushed out of plays at the NFL level due to that shortcoming if he does, in fact, make it. Still, coaches love high-energy guys like this and so Love should get his chance.

THE REST

Jarrett Johnson (Texas A @ M) 6-3 265 4.83

*Byron Cowart (Auburn) 6-4 250 4.73

Andrew Trumbetti (Notre Dame) 6-3 260 4.78

Walter Brady (Middle Tennessee) 6-3 255 4.75

DEFENSIVE TACKLES

Position Grade: A

First Round Talent: Vita Vea, Maurice Hurst, Taven Bryan, Christian Wilkins

***Taven Bryan (Florida) 6-4 291 4.99:** Undersized but speedy Florida defensive tackle Taven Bryant emerged in 2017 for the Gators after previously being a rotation player his first two years in the program. Registering 6 TFL's and 4 sacks, Bryan hints at some impactful pass rushing ability and the speed to make it through gaps before opposing lineman get fully up into their stances. Where he runs into trouble is in tight as Bryan really needs to add some weight to his 6-4 frame or else risk getting completely wiped out of plays. There is the chance that Bryan will move to defensive end at the pro level and this could really unleash his burgeoning talent. One to watch.

***Vita Vea (Washington) 6-5 332 5.20:** Run-stopping Washington defensive tackle Vita Vea will leave school a year early after receiving some fine grades from draft pundits and that is a good call since there is a strong likelihood he will hear his name called among the first two rounds. Vea is a true lane-clogging tackle who is a top-notch run defender and whose decent athleticism for such a big guy also enables him to pick up the odd sack. The power is immense and Vea also has very long arms to swat away passes at a decent clip.

Christian Wilkins (Clemson) 6-4 310 5.00: You're not going to see many D-tackles with 40-times hovering under 5.00 but that is where Clemson junior Christian Wilkins resides to raise eyebrows in the personnel community. Wilkins uses that speed to serve as a constant source of disruption and it helped lead to 4 sacks and 7 TFL's during the 2017 regular season. It is very rare where you get a tackle prospect that can beat you both with speed and strength and this is what really elevates Wilkins' standing.

Maurice Hurst (Michigan) 6-2 282 4.99: When you are discussing the speed-rushing ability of Michigan defensive tackle Maurice Hurst, it would be easy to conclude the senior would be a true first-round pick in the 2018 NFL Draft. Hurst has some uncanny explosion off the snap as he quickly fires through the gaps and gets up into the pocket to corral the passer. That led to 5.5 sacks, 13 TFL's, and a first-team selection to the All-Big Ten squad. Where things get a bit shaky center on Hurst's smallish size/frame which could neuter some of his speed advantages. The one-dimensional approach of Hurst will likely cost him that first-round slot but don't let it fool you into thinking this is not a disruptive defender.

***Da'Ron Payne (Alabama) 6-2 319 5.10:** It was Alabama junior defensive tackle Da'Ron Payne who took home Defensive Player of the Game in the Crimson Tide's championship game victory over Georgia which helped cement his decision to come out early for the draft. It was an easy call as Payne did nothing but win at Alabama where he used his wide-bodied frame and a very rare blend of speed/athleticism for someone so big. There are few players in the draft that can plug up running holes as effortlessly as Payne can and he will fight with the best of them to gain an edge. Lauded for a non-stop motor as well, Payne checks most of the boxes when it comes to being a top prospect.

*Harrison Phillips (Stanford) 6-4 285 5.24: The numbers were very impressive for Stanford junior defensive tackle Harrison Phillips in 2017 as the junior picked up 7.5 sacks and a potent 92 tackles for the team. It is rare to see so many tackles from a player who primarily plays in the middle of the defensive line but that speaks to Phillips' nose for the ball. Unfortunately, Phillips is a mediocre athlete who will have a tough go of it fighting himself free from the much bigger lineman he will face in the NFL. Phillips is lacking strength and needs to add 20 pounds at least to stick in the middle at the next level.

*Dexter Lawrence (Clemson) 6-5 340 5.20: On an absolutely loaded Clemson Tiger defense, junior tackle Dexter Lawrence might very well be the best of the bunch. That is certainly saying something considering the insane talent on those units but Lawrence certainly has the goods to back it up. A true lane clogger in every sense of the word, Lawrence swallows up running backs for lunch. Capable of shutting down opposing offenses as the nose in a 3-4 or in the middle of a 4-3, good luck trying to get Lawrence off his spot. Lawrence does have a bit of a shaky injury history but this is a future Pro Bowl-looking player if we ever saw one.

Rasheem Green (USC) 6-5 280 5.09: A move to defensive end will be in the future for USC defensive tackle Rasheem Green once he heads to the pros and for a number of reasons. Primarily speaking, Green is too small at 280 pounds to adequately maintain his position in the middle and his above-average pass rushing skills would be better suited coming off the edge in a 4-3. While he is not overly fleet of foot, Green gets off the snap in a flash and his 9 sacks from a year ago show he can make life difficult for opposing passers. Green also grades out as a solid run stopper as well which could help him secure a selection in the early rounds.

Derrick Nnadi (Florida State) 6-1 312 5.09: For all of the athleticism that Florida State defensive tackle Derrick Nnadi brought to the table, there was a sense of frustration with his overall output as a collegiate player. Blessed with terrific short-area burst and the ability to split gaps quickly, Nnadi should have been a bit more productive on the pass rushing side of things. That is a bit of a concern considering Nnadi faces some questions regarding how he will be able to make a consistent impact at the next level due to his very short 6-1 frame. While Nnadi makes up for that with speed and good power, this one could go either way.

B.J. Hill (N.C. State) 6-4 315 5.00: Swatting down passes is a bit of an art form and N.C. State defensive tackle B.J. Hill has that skill down pat. A very stout and powerful player, Hill more than did his part on a strong Wolfpack defense in 2017 with regard to greatly impeding opposing running games. Hill has very long arms which help in knocking down so many throws and he also can shed blocks impressively as well. The question is how much did Hill play off of his teammates to yield his numbers and that unknown will dip his draft slot a bit.

*Dre'Mont Jones (Ohio State) 6-3 295 4.95: While teammate Sam Hubbard got most of the press on the Ohio State defense in 2017, defensive tackle Dre'Mont Jones is not to be overlooked. When evaluating Jones, it is crucial to understand that his ability to take on two offensive linemen at the same time allowed Hubbard and company to make plays behind him. As a result, Jones' numbers don't exactly jump off the page (just one sack and 20 tackles last season). Yes, Jones is not a blue chip prospect but he has mid-round appeal as a run-stopping tackle that has the speed to occasionally slip a gap or two.

Folurunso Fatukasi (UCONN) 6-4 303 5.15: UCONN coaches had to be disappointed with the play of defensive tackle Folurunso Fatukasi the last two years after he seemed to be a star-in-the-making after putting up 7.5 sacks as a sophomore. Fatukasi has been chasing those numbers ever since and his overall production left a lot to be desired the last two seasons. It is not that Fatukasi doesn't have the tools since he has a very intriguing combination of size and speed but the numbers have not flashed for whatever reason.

Poona Ford (Texas) 6-0 310 5.02: Despite not having ideal height, Texas defensive tackle Poona Ford plays with excellent leverage to push forward into the pocket, while also using his quickness off the snap to slip the gap toward opposing passers. It is very crucial Ford continues to operate with a low center of gravity in order to hold anchor versus bigger offensive lineman and he seems capable in that regard. The short arms are a concern though and Ford's tackling was not always pretty either.

*Kendrick Norton (Miami Fla.) 6-3 318 5.19: Honorable Mention All-ACC Miami Hurricanes defensive tackle Kendrick Norton is heading to the NFL a year early and this despite being a likely mid-round pick. Norton was not a numbers guy with Miami as he picked up just 2 sacks and 23 total tackles as a junior and that will make it tough for him to stand out in a loaded position for this year's draft. The size and strength are impressive without a doubt but Norton has so far failed to move the interest meter much.

Will Geary (Kansas State) 6-0 298 5.25: Wow is this kid a monster in the weight room. Kansas State defensive tackle Will Geary has a future in strongman competitions if the NFL doesn't work out as he reportedly cleans 392 pounds, bench presses 425, and squats 640 according to an ESPN report. That is some silly strength and that alone will make Geary fully capable of locking up two offensive linemen on a given play to help free up the linebackers behind him. Geary is a classic nose tackle given his video game power but his overall size is actually a bit on the light side. With little speed to speak of, Geary will only be making an impact in stopping the run in terms of his own statistics but physically there is a lot to like here.

Andrew Brown (Virginia) 6-4 285 4.72: The size/speed quotient on Virginia defensive tackle Andrew Brown is impressive at first glance but the lack of eye-catching numbers while as a collegiate player speak to his very mediocre draft outlook. Brown doesn't really have a set position based on his physical makeup and when you throw in the average numbers, the excitement meter here doesn't go very high.

Justin Jones (N.C. State) 6-2 315 5.24: Another member of the stacked N.C. State defensive line in 2017 was tackle Justin Jones but he is taking a backseat to position mate B.J. Hill when it comes to draft interest. Now Jones is a solid player who racked up 8.5 TFL's and 2.5 sacks last season but his overall body of work makes him look like a mid-round guy. To be fair, Jones did the dirty work in terms of locking up offensive lineman so that others could make the glory plays behind him and he has the strength/size to be a lane-clogging tackle.

Lowell Lotulelei (Utah) 6-2 310 5.40: The younger brother of the Carolina Panthers' Star, Utah defensive tackle Lowell Lotulelei did his family proud by clogging up lanes at an impressive level while in college. Unfortunately, Lowell is far from the prospect Star was as he was a complete non-factor in rushing the passer and ran too hot-and-cold stopping the run. Likely looking at a late-round selection but the name will help.

*Khalil McKenzie (Tennessee) 6-3 325 5.17: The son of Oakland Raiders executive Reggie, Tennessee defensive tackle Khalil McKenzie surprised the Volunteers coaching staff by declaring early for the 2018 NFL Draft. The surprise is understandable as McKenzie is looking like a mid-to-late round pick who carries more potential than in-game production. A checkered injury history also makes McKenzie a bit of a red flag and so his massive size and strength will be what teams rely on when evaluating his draft outlook.

THE REST

Daylon Mack (Texas A @ M) 6-1 335 5.20:

Jerry Tillery (Notre Dame) 6-6 310 5.20

Drew Bailey (Louisville) 6-5 294 5.20

Bruce Hector (South Florida) 6-2 295 4.95

Matt Elam (Kentucky) 6-7 360 5.54

INSIDE LINEBACKERS

Position Grade: C+

First Round Talent: Roquon Smith

*Roquon Smith (Georgia) 6-1 225 4.57: A driving force on the championship game Georgia Bulldog squad in 2017 was without a doubt middle linebacker Roquan Smith. The leader on what became a truly dominant unit during the course of the season, Smith was a tackling machine as he became the definition of a true sideline-to-sideline linebacker. Possessing an uncanny ability to diagnose the play and get into the proper position on the field to make the tackle, Smith was a run stopping dynamo. In addition to his off-the-chart ability in the run game, Smith also had the smooth hip movement and speed to be adept at covering down the field. While he is a bit on the short side, Smith is a locked-and-loaded first round selection.

*Malik Jefferson (Texas) 6-3 238 4.68: Despite finishing the 2017 season out of commission due to a toe/leg injury, Texas middle linebacker Malik Jefferson leaves school early after a big 2017 performance that saw him rack up a massive 110 tackles, 10 TFL's, and 4 sacks. Based on the tackle numbers alone, Jefferson showed a knack for the finding the ball carrier and making the play. He also showcases textbook tackling technique and the speed to cover wide swaths of the field. The motor didn't always run at 100 percent prior to last season but Jefferson seemed to refute those concerns with his big junior campaign. As long as Jefferson continues to put in the work, he should be a high-impact player for his new team.

Rashaan Evans (Alabama) 6-3 231 4.63: So deep has been the Alabama defense under Nick Saban that it took middle linebacker Rashaan Evans making it all the way to his senior year before he became a starter. While Evans played reasonably well, he was not exactly a focal point of offenses that game planned for the Crimson Tide defense last season. Much was made of the 20.5 mile per hour velocity testing Evans underwent prior to the season's beginning and that shows the terrific amount of speed/athleticism he brings to the table. The instincts are not as potent however as Evans was often a step or two behind in diagnosing the play and coming up to make the stop. Yes, the speed allows Evans to cover a lot of ground but his school's name will inflate his standing more than it should.

Leighton Vander Esche (Boise State) 6-4 220 4.68: After hedging for weeks, Boise State middle linebacker Leighton Vander Esche declared for the 2018 NFL Draft right before the mid-January deadline. Vander Esche should be a highly coveted commodity as was an excellent sideline-to-sideline force stopping the run and there is some untapped pass rushing potential as well. Having collected 141 tackles and 4 sacks as a junior last season, Vander Esche was a fixture on the stat sheet each week for the Broncos. Physically speaking, Vander Esche has the much-desired combination of size and speed that NFL personnel gurus look for and so a Day 2 selection at worst seems to be in the cards.

Oren Burks (Vanderbilt) 6-3 230 4.72: Adept at diagnosing plays at a rapid pace is a must-have requirement to man the middle linebacker spot on a team's defense and Vanderbilt's Oren Burks certainly possesses that trait. Despite being a tad on the slow side, Burks doesn't waste steps moving into the play and making the stop with sound technique. Also possessing good size, Burks does check a lot of boxes. Where he is lacking is not being a true sideline-to-sideline guy like a Roquon Smith or a Malik Jefferson. While Burks has good range, it is not top level. He lacks a bit in the pass rushing side of things as well.

Micah Kiser (Virginia) 6-2 240 4.70: 385 tackles since 2015 was the unmatched total in all of FBS play as Virginia middle linebacker Micah Kiser cemented his status as a run-stopping force during his tenure in school. Off the snap, Kiser wastes little time finding the runner and delivers a good pop to bring his man down. Pass coverage is where the overall prospect outlook shows some leaks however as Kiser lacks the fluid change-of-direction skills and pure speed to maintain position on his man moving down the field. In fact, Kiser has truly been picked on at times to the point he may have to come off the field on passing downs. Still, Kiser has a non-stop motor and also has shown the ability to slip gaps in getting to the QB. This is an overall solid rotational player.

Dorian O'Daniel (Clemson) 6-1 220 4.54: With 99 tackles and 10.5 tackles for loss on his 2017 resume, senior Clemson linebacker Dorian O'Daniel is drawing a bunch of interest as the draft draws near. A bit under the radar coming into the year, O'Reilly really played well from the start of the season all the way to its completion in the national championship semis. Despite not being overly big, O'Daniel is very adept at getting to where he needs to go to make the play in as few steps as possible. The tackling technique is very pretty as well and O'Daniel overall seems to have really taken to coaching. There are some apparent struggles in pass coverage though and O'Daniel sometimes was blown out of plays due to his smallish size.

Darius Leonard (South Carolina State) 6-3 235 4.72: Yes it was accomplished on the small school level but South Carolina State's Darius Leonard lit up the stat sheet in racking up 113 tackles and 8 sacks as a senior in 2017. That is the type of monster production that will draw the interest of every NFL front office but of course, the question will be how much those numbers transfer to the highest level. What Leonard has going for him is an impressive game speed that allowed him to constantly wreak havoc and pick up those sacks. Where Leonard figures to run into trouble centers on his lack of strength. Leonard got by way too much on athleticism while in school and the fact he can't fall back on above-average power is a concern.

Josey Jewell (Iowa) 6-2 230 4.72: Having led the Iowa Hawkeyes in tackles each of the last three years, middle linebacker Josey Jewell has more than proven the notion he has a nose for the football. You can't teach the instincts that Jewell seems to possess as he put up an astounding 121 tackles as a senior in 2017 and validated his standing as one of the best run-stopping linebackers in the entire 2018 NFL Draft. The reason he is not ranked any higher is because of some pronounced struggles defending the pass. Jewell seems to get lost in space when out in pass coverage and he too often loses track of his man due to looking back at the passer. That red flag figures to keep Jewell as a Day 2 selection.

*Frank Ginda (San Jose State) 6-0 245 4.82: Securing first-team All-Mountain West honors likely were the impetus for San Jose State middle linebacker Frank Ginda to come out a year early in declaring for the draft but his status as a Day 3 pick seems set in stone. While Ginda is a solid overall player, he lacks the speed/athleticism needed to cover wider swaths of the field in pass defense. Be that as it may, Ginda is a terrific run defender as shown by the silly 173 tackles he accumulated in 2017. Ginda is also freakishly strong and can really lay out a ball carrier with massive hits. Could be a classic overachiever.

*Kendall Joseph (Clemson) 6-0 230 4.65: If it seems like we are constantly talking about Clemson defensive NFL draft prospects, it is because we have been. Add middle linebacker Kendall Joseph to this grouping as the junior comes out early in a year the Tigers are seemingly sending their entire 2017 defense to the pros. While Joseph is a productive player (124 tackles last season), his NFL ceiling is that of a middle round pick due to some struggles defending the pass and also for lacking in size. The tackle numbers do show that Joseph diagnoses the play well but there are warts around the edges of his game.

Shaun Dion Hamilton (Alabama) 6-0 232 4.63: The medical chart on Alabama linebacker Shaun Dion Hamilton looks like it is right out of an episode of Grey's Anatomy and that certainly won't help him when it comes to the draft process. A torn ACL in 2016 was soon followed by a November cracked patella that ended his season early. In between all of the medical chaos, Hamilton is quite disruptive due to his speed-centric game slipping into the opposing team's backfield at a high rate. The range is impressive as well and Hamilton can defend the pass adequately. The height is not ideal and Hamilton could use some more muscle on his frame but the medical report will ultimately win out in terms of where he gets drafted.

Nick DeLuca (North Dakota State) 6-3 245 4.82: Small-school middle linebacker Nick DeLuca is hoping to land as a Day 3 pick despite the fact he has been constantly injured during his collegiate career. A serious shoulder injury knocked him out for 2016 and an early knee scare last season thankfully turned out to be minor. In terms of on-the-field work, DeLuca is a play-to-the-whistle linebacker who can pack a punch. Possessing above-average strength, DeLuca's tackling fundamentals are solid and he is adept at making plays in the run game. He is another big-bodied linebacker who struggles in pass protection, however; with a lack of pure athleticism serving as the main issue regarding his struggle on that side of the offensive attack.

Jack Cincy (Wisconsin) 6-2 233 4.77: A torn ACL in fall camp finished Wisconsin middle linebacker Jack Cincy before he could even play one snap in 2017 but he decided not to take a medical redshirt in order to enter the 2018 NFL Draft. Lauded as a solid prospect prior to the injury, Cincy has to answer some medical questions before his status again rises in the draft. Prior to the injury, Cincy was a textbook tackling linebacker who overcome a lack of pure speed with smart awareness and an ability to read the play. Cincy is a bit one-dimensional as he didn't flash much when it came to rushing the passer but the talent is still there underneath the medical reports.

Matthew Thomas (Florida State) 6-2 227 4.60: Athletically speaking, Florida State middle linebacker Matthew Thomas has all the tools needed to be a high-impact player. From top-end speed for the position to impressive pure strength, Thomas is an athletic marvel. Unfortunately, all those skills need to be complemented by the mental side of things and that is where the trouble arises. Thomas was often a step or two slow off the snap in reading the play and he habitually tackled with a grabbing approach instead of properly wrapping up. The latter can be addressed through coaching but the former is a problem that can seriously undermine any defensive player.

Azeem Victor (Washington) 6-4 232 4.78: It was a pretty ugly last two years in Washington for middle linebacker Azeem Victor, to say the least. First, he missed virtually the entire 2016 season with a broken leg and 2017 brought a three-game suspension due to being arrested for a DUI. Character concerns aside, Victor played poorly for large stretches of the season as he was robotic in his movements and lacked the speed to cover a high amount of ground.

THE REST

Keishawn Bierria (Washington) 6-1 223 4.75

Chad Whitener (Oklahoma State) 6-0 248 4.65:

Nyles Morgan (Notre Dame) 6-1 245 4.74

Taylor Young (Baylor) 5-10 225 4.63

OUTSIDE LINEBACKERS

Position Grade: B-

First Round Talent: Tremaine Edmunds, Ogbonnia Okoronkwo

*Tremaine Edmunds (Virginia Tech) 6-5 238 4.71: With Kentucky's Josh Allen deciding to head back to school for 2018, the mantle of being the top outside linebacker in the upcoming NFL Draft likely belongs to Virginia Tech's Tremaine Edmunds. Edmunds has some freakish athletic talent that is highlighted by very impressive strength and pure speed. That speed has helped Edmunds put up over 100 tackles each of the last two seasons and also enabled him to be a constant source of disruption for opposing QB's. Checking both the run-stopping and pass rushing boxes, Edmunds will be a hot property on Day 1 of the draft.

Ogbonnia Okoronkwo (Oklahoma) 6-1 242 4.69: Having won the Big 12 Defensive Player of the Year award, Oklahoma outside linebacker Ogbonnia Okoronkwo certainly heads into the NFL Draft on a high note. A late bloomer who barely played as a sophomore, Okoronkwo racked up 8 sacks and a staggering 17 tackles for a loss in 2017. Clearly, Okoronkwo was very disruptive to opposing offenses and he is certainly peaking at the right time in moving toward being a first-round pick this spring. Possessing very long arms and excellent speed, Okoronkwo is an athletic marvel who will be a major force off the edge at the pro level. The one concern we do have with Okoronkwo is that he is on the small side at 6-1 and he will likely face his fair share of being completely blocked out of the play if he gets too in tight with a blocker.

Lorenzo Carter (Georgia) 6-6 242 4.75: Serving as perhaps a bit of an enigma, Georgia outside linebacker Lorenzo Carter does hint at some big-time ability. The problem is that he often struggled to stay consistent and he seemed more capable than just the 4 sacks he had a year ago. The tools are there to be coached up however as Carter plays with a toughness/determination to get up the field. He is also capable of gaining separation both with his speed and power. One of the more interesting Day 2/3 prospects.

*James Hearns (Louisville) 6-3 249 4.65: With 7 sacks and 13.5 tackles for loss in 2017, Louisville outside linebacker James Hearns goes into the NFL Draft with a good chance of being a Day 2 pick. While not as dynamic as Tremaine Edmunds, Hearns does possess his own impressive brand of pass-rushing ability and a non-stop motor to make life miserable for opposing passers. Hearns can get the edge with a rapid first step and he has also shown good counter moves as well if stunted initially. Just an average run stopper, Hearns will make his money by what he does in terms of getting into the backfield. On that front, he looks to be quite capable.

*Jerome Baker (Ohio State) 6-1 225 4.55: Another early entry from the Ohio State Buckeyes into the 2018 NFL Draft is outside linebacker Jerome Baker. While there is always a bit of an extra bit of respect given to players from big programs, Baker will likely be more of a Day 2 prospect than a Day 1. On the positive side, Baker has been lauded for his impressive work in pass coverage. Baker relies on his excellent speed to shadow receivers and runners coming out of the backfield and with the NFL being a big aerial show, this is a crucial skill. On the negative side, Baker is an inconsistent run stopper who often got pushed out of the play due to a strength shortcoming.

*Jeff Holland (Auburn) 6-2 249 4.76: One outside linebacker who should be placed firmly in the "pass rushing specialist" tier is Auburn's Jeff Holland. Picking up 9 sacks as a junior, Holland explodes off the snap and can be a nightmare for tackles that require an extra second to get into position. Holland also gets his hand on the football at a high rate, causing four fumbles a year ago as well. The problem here is that Holland can be neutralized if he can't get the edge right away as he lacks length and size. He also is a below-average performer in stopping the run which eliminates him as an every down linebacker.

Sione Teuhema (Southeast Louisiana) 6-4 245 4.70: A former LSU Tiger who transferred to Southeast Louisiana, Sione Teuhema is toughness personified. Playing with a nasty streak, Teuhema picked up 80 tackles and 9 sacks in 2017. In terms of that toughness we talked about, Teuhema gets 90 percent of his numbers through pure power and excellent hand-to-hand skills. Keep in mind that Teuhema is a bit of a hothead who caught a suspension at the end of 2015 that went into spring ball the following year for an unknown reason.

Skai Moore (South Carolina) 6-2 218 4.59: The utter lack of size for South Carolina outside linebacker Skai Moore becomes the main storyline here as he constantly fought injuries in college and holding up to NFL pounding will be a giant challenge. It is imperative Moore operates at outside linebacker because he needs the space to use his excellent speed to gain an edge on offensive tackles or to come up and make an unencumbered stop in the run game. A serious neck injury in 2016 speaks to the unreliability of Moore physically and that will keep him cemented as a mid-round pick.

Uchenna Nwosu (USC) 6-2 240 4.75: Like with Skai Moore, USC's Uchenna Nwosu has some size challenges that will hurt his NFL Draft stock. In space, Nwosu is adept at coming up to make the tackle and generate a rush. He did pick up 7.5 sacks as a senior in 2017 which speak to his pass rushing ability but he also too often gets swallowed whole by the bigger offensive lineman. Trustworthy in pass coverage, Nwosu has enough pure skill to be worthy of Day 3 status.

Davin Bellamy (Georgia) 6-5 240 4.78: Despite playing high-visibility games for the Georgia Bulldogs in 2017, outside linebacker Davin Bellamy is just an average NFL prospect. Bellamy seems to lack a true position and he has a poor pass rushing game. Bellamy mostly did his work stopping the run and also using his long arms to force fumbles/knock down passes. The name brand could help him in the draft but Bellamy should be a firm Day 3 pick.

Mike McCray (Michigan) 6-4 248 4.68: Boy if Michigan outside linebacker Mike McCray could burn the tape against Penn State this past season, he would be wise to do so. McCray was simply brutal in that one as he got beaten and abused all game long by Nittany Lions running back Saquon Barkley. While Barkley made a lot of defenders look silly last season, McCray's big-time struggles in pass coverage and stopping the run was obvious. McCray was previously lauded for his impressive ability to generate a rush and while that still holds true, the fact he has an incomplete game will hurt him in the draft.

*Te'Von Coney (Notre Dame) 6-1 235 4.73: A bright spot on a somewhat inconsistent Notre Dame defense in 2017 was outside linebacker Te'Von Coney who amassed 99 tackles, 12.5 TFL's, and 3 sacks as a junior. Coney decided that was enough to leave the Irish a year early but he will likely be just a middle-round pick due to size/speed concerns. What Coney has going for him is possessing good awareness of the play and a quick read off the snap. He can fight his way free from blocks as well but Coney also struggles to generate pressure off the edge due to being a bit slow off the snap.

Fred Warner (BYU) 6-4 230 4.78: Yes there is not much of a pass rushing game to speak of when evaluating BYU outside linebacker Fred Warner (just two total sacks the last two seasons combined) but it is apparent there is in fact some interesting run-stopping ability here. Warner seemed to always be around the football on that side of things as a senior and that will help secure him a rotational spot as a Day 3 pick.

Jason Cabinda (Penn State) 6-1 232 4.75: One of our favorite "rising" prospects as of this writing is Penn State outside linebacker Jason Cabinda. While he didn't get much national hype, Cabinda had an excellent/vastly underrated senior season that included 86 tackles, 3.5 sacks, 6 TFL's, and 3 passes batted away. In other words, Cabinda did a little of everything and at the very least, he should have three-down potential as a pro. Now Cabinda is more of a run-stopper than a pure pass rusher which could necessitate a move to the inside but this is a potentially big hidden gem of a player who needs to be on most personnel lists as a mid-round target.

Chris Worley (Ohio State) 6-2 230 4.70: Ohio State linebacker Chris Worley is an experienced player who has worked extensively both on the outside and inside. His senior year was spent on the inside where he played solid but unspectacular football. Worley lacks a signature skill that will get him out of the late rounds of the draft but he has enough talent to get a long look as a contributor from a major college program.

THE REST

Reggie Carter (Georgia)

Tre' Williams (Auburn)

*Christian Williams (Alabama)

Jacob Pugh (Florida State)

STRONG SAFETY

Position Grade: B-

First Round Talent: Derwin James

***Derwin James (Florida State) 6-3 211 4.50:** First-Team All-ACC Florida State safety Derwin James looks set to be a top 15 pick in the 2018 NFL Draft and that standing is well-earned. James is a classic do-it-all strong safety who has exceptional range and can really lay the wood on wideouts. Blessed with very good speed and the ability to change direction on a dime, James has tremendous range all over the field. Better yet, James seems to be sound physically after missing almost all of 2016 with a knee injury. The one knock on James is that he struggles to keep up with some of the more shifty/speedy wideouts but that is a major nitpick.

***Ronnie Harrison (Alabama) 6-3 216 4.53:** It is almost unfair that the Alabama Crimson Tide were able to trot out both Ronnie Harrison and Minkah Fitzpatrick on a weekly basis at the safety position this past season. While Fitzpatrick excelled in pass coverage (and pretty much everything else), it was apparent that Harrison was much more adept as a run stopper and a roaming big-hitter in the middle of the field. Harrison had some major problems when asked to cover slot wideouts this past season and that struggle will likely push him down toward the bottom of Round 1 and more likely into Round 2. Still, Harrison was every bit the leader Fitzpatrick was on the national champions and good luck going across the middle with him lurking.

***Jordan Whitehead (Pittsburgh) 5-11 190 4.45:** Some superb athleticism at the safety position can be found in the form of Pittsburgh's Jordan Whitehead. Whitehead is a bit of a unique player in that in addition to manning his safety spot, the Pitt coaching staff also used him some at running back. That makes sense since Whitehead has track speed with a 4.45 time in the 40. The speed is needed since Whitehead is vertically challenged and has some clear issues covering bigger receivers. Attitude/discipline is up for debate as well since Whitehead earned a three-game suspension from the team at the start of 2017.

Damon Webb (Ohio State) 5-11 195 4.50: Former four-star Ohio State safety recruit Damon Webb generally had a solid career with the Buckeyes as he heads into the 2018 NFL Draft. Webb picked off four passes and knocked down 3 others as a senior in 2017 which sets him up as a mid-round pick. The reason Webb won't likely hear his name called on the first two days of the draft is due to a short and very slight frame that will lead to trouble against bigger NFL receivers. Webb is always willing to throw his body around and tackles well but he looks more suited to a nickel role as a pro.

Siran Neal (Jacksonville State) 6-1 205 4.57: Small-school combo safety/cornerback Siran Neal is another classic case of top-end athleticism always garnering attention in the draft community. Neal's measurables are beyond impressive as he can run like the wind and also deliver a big hit. Clearly, Neal will be a work in progress given the vast step up in quality of competition but at the very least he can start at nickel cornerback and work his way up from there.

Tray Matthews (Auburn) 6-1 209 4.50: Previously unheralded Auburn safety Tray Matthews put himself on the prospect map with a nice senior campaign where he collected 59 tackles, one INT, and two passes batted away. Not spectacular numbers by any means but Matthews is a heavy hitter who does a nice job both stopping the run and in pass coverage. Speed is Matthews' best asset but his tackling needs work and he tends to surrender completions versus slot receivers.

Marcus Allen (Penn State) 6-2 205 4.63: Lauded for strong run-stopping work, Penn State strong safety Marcus Allen looks poised to be a mid-round pick this spring. Allen comes up to the line of scrimmage with authority and delivers a forceful hit to any runner who comes into his range. Allen does struggle to stay with opposing receivers in pass coverage though and that is mainly due to his mediocre speed. Noticeably picked on in some games last season, Allen needs to get into the classroom to shore up that obvious weakness. If not, he is likely going to be nothing but a backup for his NFL squad.

Jonathan Abram (Mississippi State) 6-0 210 4.56: 71 tackles as a senior highlight the statistical package for Mississippi State safety Jonathan Abram in 2017. While he had some run-ins with the school/coaching staff in 2016, Abram kept quiet as a senior and had a very solid season stopping the run in picking up 71 tackles. Struggles covering wideouts was a decent-sized negative however and Abram's measurables have him mostly as a Day 3 pick.

Godwin Igwebuike (Northwestern) 6-0 200 4.59: An intriguing Day 3 safety pick looks to be Northwestern's Godwin Igwebuike on the strength of some impressive tackling numbers while in school. Igwebuike has a vast amount of experience as a guy who contributed all four years he was in the program and his highlight was accumulating 108 tackles and 2 picks as a junior. While his senior year was a bit less eye-opening, Igwebuike makes the most of his limited athletic ability to always be around the football. Some issues in coverage need to be worked out but the kid looks like a player.

Tre Flowers (Oklahoma State) 6-3 200 4.57: A bit stiff in his movements and possessing an overly lanky frame, Oklahoma State safety Tre Flowers is set to be nothing more than a Day 3 pick in this year's draft. Where Flowers is a decent asset is in stopping the run as he has picked up 79 and 83 tackles the last two seasons. A vastly experienced player, Flowers can be a backup safety at the next level.

THE REST

Steven Parker (Oklahoma) 6-1 201 4.63

Cole Reyes (North Dakota) 6-2 215 4.54

Nick Washington (Florida) 6-0 205 4.57

Tyree Robinson (Oregon) 6-4 205 4.64

Jarod Franklin (Tulane) 6-0 205 4.57

Trey Marshall (Florida State) 6-0 210 4.58

FREE SAFETY

Position Grade: A-

First Round Talent Minkah Fitzpatrick, Terrell Edmunds

*Minkah Fitzpatrick (Alabama) 6-1 203 4.55: Joining Florida State's Derwin James as an early first-round safety in the upcoming 2018 NFL Draft will undoubtedly be Alabama's Minkah Fitzpatrick. The free safety dynamo is one of the best cover safeties to come out in years; capable of sticking with tight ends, slot men, or deep-play wideouts all over the field. Fitzpatrick has great fluidity in his hips and those movements help him perform lockdown coverage duties. What really makes Fitzpatrick the total package is that he is also an above-average defender in the run game. Yes Fitzpatrick is not the hitter James is but his tackling is flawless. A true star-in-the-making.

*DeShon Elliott (Texas) 6-2 210 4.58: A true ball hawk of a safety can be found in Texas where junior DeShon Elliott picked off six passes for the Longhorns in 2017 to stamp his reputation for excellence there. Elliott comes out early after making plays all over the secondary for Texas, adding 63 tackles and 3 batted down passes for good measure. Elliott can be a bit too aggressive in coverage going for those picks; with more than a few occasions occurring where he bit on fakes and in the process surrendered long completions. The discipline needs some shoring up but love the can-do attitude. Pure coverage ability is just average minus the turnovers but Elliott makes his presence felt.

*Terrell Edmunds (Virginia Tech) 6-2 220 4.58: There may not be a more proud football mom than the matriarch of the Edmunds family. Not only will mom see outside linebacker son Trumaine head to the NFL this upcoming April but he will be joined by free safety son Terrell. The Virginia Tech junior leaves school early after a solid 2017 campaign where Terrell showcased some impressive coverage skills. Capable of patrolling wide swaths of the field, Terrell picked off four passes last season and constantly was around the football. He has been somewhat inconsistent coming up to stop the run due to some indecisiveness and false steps but the effort is always there.

*Justin Reid (Stanford) 6-1 204 4.53: The brother of the NFL's Eric, Stanford free safety Justin Reid should keep the family name active in the league as he likely will hear his name called among the first two days of the draft. Reid comes off a splendid junior season where he accumulated 99 tackles, 6 passes defended, and five INT's to make his decision to come out early an easy one. Better suited to strong safety due to some pass coverage struggles, Reid is a big-hitter whose textbook tackling makes him a run stopping weapon.

Quin Blanding (Virginia) 6-1 215 4.62: Take a look at the tackle numbers accumulated by Virginia free safety Quin Blanding and no doubt your eyes will open wide. Each of the last three seasons has seen Blanding collect more than 100 tackles which is a very rare total for a safety and it speaks to how good of a tackler the senior is. This past season was no different as Blanding led all safeties in college football in tackles with 121. As great as Blanding is in the run game, he is equally brutal in pass coverage. Blanding takes poor angles in pass protection and he often has trouble keeping up with pure speed slot guys. Picked on liberally at times, Blanding will likely have to come off the field on passing downs given his ongoing struggles there.

Armani Watts (Texas A @ M) 5-11 196 4.65: Texas A @ M free safety Armani Watts is an interesting player in that he collected a ton of numbers during his stint with the Aggies but whose lack of desired height/size for an NFL defensive back is lacking. While Watts did have his hands full handling bigger wideouts, he also never backed down in sticking his nose into the play. That resulted in Watts becoming the only active FBS player in 2017 to have 300 tackles, 10 interceptions, and five forced fumbles according to ESPN. Those are some crazy numbers and it shows Watts is one of those classic players who make the most of his ability. Keep in mind though that Watts also has a very checkered injury history and his smaller size could continue that trend.

Dominick Sanders (Georgia) 6-0 189 4.58: When looking at the tape on senior Georgia safety Dominick Sanders, the ball skills quickly jump out. Sanders can read passing plays very well and he has the technique/speed to stick to most wideouts. This enabled Sanders to pick up 4 INTs' and 3 passes batted down in 2017 and that strength is what will make him a Day 3 pick. That will have to be the case as Sanders is a below-average run stopper who can't hold up physically when engaged in tight with a blocker given his slight frame.

Trayvon Henderson (Hawaii) 6-0 200 4.50: While very small in size/strength, Hawaii free safety Trayvon Henderson is a possible Day 3 option given his terrific range in coverage. Henderson can really run and has fluid hip movements in coverage to grade out highly there. On the flip side, Henderson is very small and likely will have to be a nickel cornerback initially. He is a liability stopping the run as Henderson is easily cast aside given his small stature and that keeps the ceiling quite limited.

Jeremy Reaves (South Alabama) 5-11 205 4.54: Yet another small school safety is well on the NFL radar in the form of South Alabama's Jeremy Reaves who has put up some tremendous numbers at the lower level. Reaves earned the Sun Belt Defensive Player of the Year award after picking up 104 tackles, 7 TFL's, and 3 interceptions and so it is apparent he has a nose for the football. Really like the way Reaves wraps up the ball carrier with textbook technique and he sticks well with slot receivers as well. The trouble arrives when Reaves has to come up to make stops in the run game as his lack of size hurts him on that front. Still, the kid deserves a long look.

Natrell Jamerson (Wisconsin) 6-0 198 4.54: Wisconsin senior Natrell Jamerson has been all over the playing map as he came to the school as a wide receiver, then moved to cornerback, and then finally stuck at safety where he played as a starter as a senior. Jamerson has immense athletic talent which is why he is able to play multiple positions and he also excelled as a kick returner as well. Clearly, Jamerson can run and his coverage ability plays off that skill. He is still quite raw though and Jamerson lacks in fundamentals with regards to tackling and reading the play.

Van Smith (Clemson) 5-11 195 4.60: Clemson safety Van Smith heads into the draft season on a bit of a down note. After opening eyes as a junior and first-time starter on the Tigers, Smith took a step back through some struggles as a senior in 2017. Smith really hurt his stock by becoming a liability in pass coverage and he routinely struggled to contain taller receivers given the fact he stands under 6-foot. While you like the speed aspect of his game, Smith is going to face an uphill battle being more than a nickel back/rotational safety in the pros.

Jamaar Summers (UCONN) 6-0 190 4.56: Capable of playing either safety or cornerback, UCONN's Jamaar Summers will rely on his above-average coverage skills to get him a look from an NFL team. Having picked off as many as 8 passes in a season (when he was a sophomore), Summers knows what he needs to do in pass coverage. Shoddy work on the run game and a question mark about where he will play will follow Summers to the NFL.

THE REST

*Jaleel Wadwood (UCLA) 5-10 175 4.69

Drue Tranquill (Notre Dame) 6-1 225 4.65

Ed Parris (LSU) 6-0 210 4.54

Donnie Miles (North Carolina) 5-11 210 4.62

Evan Berry (Tennessee) 5-11 207 4.62

CORNERBACK

Position Grade: A

First Round Talent: Joshua Jackson, Denzel Ward, Isaiah Oliver, Kameron Kelly

*Joshua Jackson (Iowa) 6-1 192 4.51: When you are considered to be the top prospect among the deepest position in an entire draft, that says something about the type of talent we are talking about here. Such is the status of Iowa cornerback Joshua Jackson who goes into the 2018 NFL Draft with the mantle of being the top dog at that particular spot and he should not be waiting around long before hearing his name called on Day 1. In terms of ability, Jackson is a true shutdown cornerback who picked off a massive 8 passes and knocked down 20 others in a spectacular 2017 performance. What makes Jackson such a premier prospect is that not only does he possess top-end speed, he also has the size to cover most receivers in any situation. Get set for a lot of Pro Bowls here.

*Denzel Ward (Ohio State) 5-10 191 4.48: While he is a bit shorter than Iowa's Josh Jackson, Ohio State cornerback Denzel Ward is very much a shutdown cornerback as well. Possessing explosive speed, Ward has excellent instincts and fluidity in his movements to shadow receivers very effectively. Ward's overall athleticism is off the charts and he can contribute right away as a returner if need be as well. About the only quibble one may have here is that Ward doesn't get his hands on as many balls as Jackson (2 INT's and 15 passes batted last season) but that shouldn't prevent him from being a first-round pick.

*Isaiah Oliver (Colorado) 6-1 190 4.55: A track star at Colorado in addition to his football duties, Isaiah Oliver is one of the best athletes in the entire NFL Draft. He caught a bunch of attention during this past season when ESPN's Mel Kiper rated Oliver the number 1 cornerback prospect for the 2018 draft but truth be told, the junior did pop as much as anticipated. With just two interceptions and 25 tackles, Oliver left some plays on the field. He obviously runs well given the track background which of course helps in coverage but Oliver gave up a few more completions than you would like. Clearly, there are a ton of tools to work with and Oliver has a precious combo of size and speed to be a future star. However, he didn't exactly look like that player with the Buffaloes.

Kameron Kelly (San Diego State) 6-2 200 4.57: What a senior season San Diego State's Kameron Kelly had. Not only did Kelly rack up 68 tackles and 8 passes knocked down, he also threw in 3 picks and 2 sacks for good measure. Kelly is a very tough and physical corner who used every bit of his size advantage to make life hell for opposing wideouts. It is imperative that Kelly use this approach due to the fact he has below-average speed for the position and in particular has trouble with deep-play receivers.

*Carlton Davis (Auburn) 6-1 195 4.53: Auburn star cornerback Carlton Davis is coming out a year early but he has three years of experience already under his belt in the always brutal SEC. That is about as tremendous a prep as a cornerback can get considering the immense quality of competition in the league and so Davis is likely going to be a hit-the-ground-running prospect who can help right away. What we really like about Davis is his willingness to mix it up and he grades out very highly in terms of fighting for the football in tight. He does lack top-end speed however and that leads to some problems defending the more speedy wideouts.

*Donte Jackson (LSU) 5-11 175 4.45: LSU cornerback Donte Jackson certainly has the speed aspect down pat for the position and that skills really complements him as a very good cover guy. Jackson can clearly run with any receiver out there but he is a bit on the short side at 5-11. That becomes an issue in jump ball scenarios or around the red zone but Jackson is always willing to fight for the ball. Penalties were a problem though and Jackson also tends to bite too often on play fakes. If he learns some more discipline, Jackson has the talent to be an impressive player.

*Mike Hughes (Central Florida) 5-11 185 4.50: The undefeated Central Florida Knights got a big boost in their secondary from big-play cornerback Mike Hughes. Hughes correctly declared early for the 2018 NFL Draft after a junior campaign that saw him pick off four passes, while also averaging a robust 31.8 yards on kick returns (including two touchdowns). It is obvious that Hughes' greatest strength is his amazing speed and there are few wideouts he can't run stride-for-stride with. What really is a plus here as well is the fact that Davis showed an impressive ability to make up ground if he fell a step or two behind in coverage. What Davis does need to work on is using his hands more. He also tends to look back a bit too much at the QB and that can lead to his man getting away from him in pass coverage.

*Jaire Alexander (Louisville) 5-11 188 4.42: It was a bit of a tough of it for junior Louisville corner Jaire Alexander in 2017 as he managed to play in just six games due to a knee injury and a broken hand. While you would have liked to have seen more film on someone coming out early, Alexander on the surface appears to be a highly capable player who showcases some impressive ball skills. Alexander is one of the fastest players in the entire draft no matter the position and so he has no issue shadowing any receiver down the field. Outside of durability concerns, there is a question regarding how Alexander will handle the bigger possession wideouts he will see in the NFL. Alexander is not a guy who seems to want to grapple much and his tackling is underwhelming.

*Nick Wilson (Wisconsin) 5-11 204 4.54: Wisconsin cornerback Nick Wilson is yet another from the position who is coming out early but he has a nice batch of experience both with the Badgers and during his earlier stint at Hawaii. Wilson does an excellent job maintaining positioning on receivers and in particular, uses his body to force his foe toward the sideline which takes out windows for the QB to throw into. The hands are also very potent here as Wilson knocked down 20 balls last season. The problem is that he failed to intercept one single pass last season and that is a knock he has to fix at the pro level. Ultimately, that will likely push Wilson to Day 2 status.

*J.C. Jackson (Maryland) 6-1 193 4.49: If you were to grade Maryland cornerback J.C. Jackson on ability alone, he might have been able to sneak into the late Day 1 picture. Unfortunately, athletic skill is only part of the equation here as Jackson was kicked out of the Florida Gators program after being charged in an armed robbery and four total felonies in the incident. While Jackson was eventually acquitted, the whole ordeal has stained him to this day in terms of the draft. After transferring to Maryland, Jackson stayed out of trouble and let his skills do the talking. On that front, Jackson was very good as he showed a very rare and highly attractive combination of size and speed to hint at a big future as an NFL cornerback. Jackson has no fear in coverage and throws a good jam off the line. He also has excellent speed and quickness in coverage. What is lacking on the field is discipline (which is ironic) as Jackson is a gambler and also tends to freelance some. He also has a bit of a durability question mark as well since he has a shoulder surgery in his past.

*Sam Beal (Western Michigan) 6-1 185 4.51: It really is amazing how many top cornerback prospects are coming out of school early and that means some will see their stock drop a bit further than expected given the glut. That could happen to Western Michigan's Sam Beal who had a very solid career in college but who lacks the flash of some of the guys ranked ahead of him. Be that as it may, Beal has decent cover skills and is an excellent tackler. He gets beaten from time-to-time on pump fakes and is overly grabby at times in tight but Beal has untapped potential.

*Tarvarus McFadden (Florida State) 6-2 198 4.52: When evaluating the collegiate career of Florida State junior cornerback Tarvarus McFadden, the inconsistency was apparent. After intercepting 8 passes as a sophomore, McFadden failed to pick off one single throw last season. On the positive side, you have to love the size here as McFadden is quite tall and has long arms to really lock up opposing wideouts. Change-of-direction skills are just all right and McFadden needs to stop peeking in so much into the backfield. Otherwise, there is a nice array of skills here that could develop in time.

Duke Dawson (Florida) 5-10 200 4.53: At the very least, Florida cornerback Duke Dawson certainly learned a lot playing previously with NFL draftees Teez Tabor and Quincy Wilson. Dawson showed evidence of this by playing a technically sound cornerback position for the Gators in 2017 but he also was inconsistent from game-to-game. While Dawson has solid straight line speed, he loses a step when forced to change direction and he was beaten over the top a bit too much for our liking. In actuality, Dawson will be best served to learn for a year as a backup before transitioning into a starter.

Adonis Alexander (Virginia Tech) 6-3 193 4.51: As of this writing it was not known if Virginia Tech corner Adonis Alexander would come out early but if he did, his 6-3 height will take on a lot of attention. Alexander has a wide wingspan that helps him engulf wideouts and he is overly physical as well. Where Alexander struggles in when he is asked to cover quicker and more shift wideouts. Alexander doesn't change direction very well in terms of maintaining speed and he also doesn't always make the right read either. Finally, Alexander caught a two-game suspension by the team at the end of 2016 for a violation of team rules which could call into question the kid's judgment.

*Kevin Toliver II (LSU) 6-2 193 4.54: Physical LSU corner Kevin Toliver comes out a year early but the reception on him is a bit mixed. What Toliver does do well is throw a good jam on the receiver off the snap and he is a big hitter who also tackles well. The downside is that Toliver gave up too many completions last season and his overall cover skills are hit-and-miss.

Christian Campbell (Penn State) 6-1 194 4.56: If Penn State cornerback Christian Campbell can nail his 40-time at the combine, he could really shoot up some draft charts. Despite some average pure speed, Campbell used his 6-1 height to constantly get his hands on the football (12 passes batted down last season) and he used a physical/hard-hitting approach to get opposing wideouts something to think about. Having shown the ability to also come up and make stops in the run game, there is a lot to work with here. Of course, Campbell has to answer the speed questions and if he can successfully deal with the DeSean Jackson's of the world.

*D.J. Reed (Kansas State) 6-1 194 4.56: First-Team All-Big Ten cornerback selection D.J. Reed will exit Kansas State a year early after putting up 47 tackles, 9 passes batted down, and four picks as a junior. Those are some tidy numbers and as an added bonus, Reed also averaged a potent 34.2 yards per kickoff return. While Reed certainly has a lot to offer, he has to answer some coverage questions as was a bit inconsistent there in 2017. Yes, Reed got his hands on a high amount of passes but he also surrendered a bunch of completions as well. Nickel back duties await him initially but anything more is up for debate.

M.J. Stewart (North Carolina) 5-11 190 4.57: North Carolina cornerback M.J. Stewart was a rare bright spot on the brutal Tar Heels football team last season and the skill level here could result in a Day 2 selection if all breaks right. Stewart is a tough and physical corner who doesn't like to yield an inch without a fight and he also showcased a knack for coming up and making stops in the run game. Hip movement and change-of-direction skills are lacking a bit, while Stewart's speed is a bit below where you would like a corner to be. There are leadership qualities here in terms of Stewart performing so well for North Carolina last season despite how brutal the team was and this should count as an added bonus.

*Quenton Meeks (Stanford) 6-1 195 4.53: It is a bit questionable the decision Stanford cornerback Quenton Meeks made to come out early this year but there is no denying the kid has a nose for the football as he picked off 7 passes combined the last two seasons. While he does gamble a bit too much, Meeks can run with almost all wideouts stride-for-stride and at the same time, uses his long arms to swat down a high number of passes. He can be beaten over the top though and penalties added up here. Still a bit too raw to think Meeks is deserving of a Day 2 grade.

Tony Brown (Alabama) 6-0 195 4.52: There wasn't much going on when it came to Alabama senior cornerback Tony Brown in 2017. While you obviously have to have the skill to play on a Nick Saban defense, Brown was vastly inconsistent during his time in Tuscaloosa and he also dealt with numerous injuries. The latter included a knee sprain that dogged Brown during the postseason and his overall numbers (0 INT, 2 passes batted, 36 tackles) left a lot to be desired.

Danny Johnson (Southern) 5-9 185 4.40: Oh my goodness the athleticism is ridiculous when you take a look at Southern cornerback Danny Johnson. This small school hidden gem has Olympic speed and he also played wide receiver and was a returner in addition to Johnson's cornerback duties to show some terrific versatility. Of course, Johnson had to go the small school route due to his incredibly short and lanky frame but at the very least, the kid can make it initially as a nickel corner and a return man as a pro.

Blace Brown (Troy) 6-0 186 4.54: One player who really helped his draft stock in 2017 was Troy corner Blace Brown. Brown was a force in pass coverage as he picked off four throws, knocked down 6 others, and forced a fumble. Those are some impressive ball skills for a smaller school player and it brings some much-deserved attention. Be that as it may, Brown is not overly quick and he will have to rely more on physicality and instincts to gain an edge on wideouts.

Jaylen Dunlap (Illinois) 6-1 190 4.45: Despite not playing much as a starter in college, Illinois cornerback Jaylen Dunlap has an eye-opening combination of size and speed that should get him a Day 3 look. Dunlap can really run and working as a return man right away while learning how to play corner at the pro level is a possibility. Dunlap has to get into the classroom as he made just 9 starts as a senior and was just all right in terms of performance.

Taron Johnson (Weber State) 6-0 175 4.51: Being the first Weber State player since 1989 to participate in the Senior Bowl is quite an accomplishment in and of itself for cornerback Taron Johnson but the kid has some skills to offer to the NFL as well. Also garnering the 2017 Big Sky Defensive Player of the Year award, Johnson knows what he is doing in pass coverage in picking off 3 passes and knocking down 8 others in 2017. He will have to face the typical learning curve that comes from making the jump to the pros from the small school level but don't count this one out.

*Holton Hill (Texas) 6-3 200 4.57: A failed drug test and the subsequent three-game suspension was not the way Texas cornerback Holton Hill wanted to end his collegiate career. That grand act of stupidity will surely dog Hill as he heads into the 2018 NFL Draft and rightfully so. The real shame of it all is that Hill has some very intriguing ability as a very tall corner can be a real handful for opposing wideouts. There is a lack of fluidity in Hill's movements and his tackling was just average. The bigger issue though is getting his head on straight and for now, we have no clue if Hill is capable of doing so.

Chandon Sullivan (Georgia State) 5-11 195 4.54: All-Sun Belt Honorable Mention Georgia State cornerback Chandon Sullivan opened enough eyes to earn a Senior Bowl invite leading into the 2018 NFL Draft and so he will have a prime opportunity to show what he can do against better competition. That is the big unknown with guys like Sullivan from a smaller program but he grades out athletically with impressive speed and admirable coverage ability.

Jalen Davis (Utah State) 5-10 185 4.54: An FBS-tying 5 interceptions in 2017 will be the calling card for Utah State cornerback Jalen Davis going into the upcoming draft. Davis was a human missile in the Utah State secondary last season as he also broke up 15 passes and showcased terrific coverage ability. The step up in competition will be daunting for Davis but he can grab hold of a nickel job if he plays well in the Senior Bowl.

Levi Wallace (Alabama) 6-0 170 4.58: Former Alabama walk-on cornerback Levi Wallace may actually get to hear his name called on Day 3 of the NFL Draft considering how nicely he developed under Nick Saban. While clearly a bit player on the Crimson Tide defense in 2017 compared to his blue-chip teammates on that side of the ball, Wallace still did his part in picking up 3 picks, 2 sacks, and 4.5 tackles for loss. Unfortunately, Wallace is simply too slow and slight in frame to make it as a starter in the NFL.

Kamrin Moore (Boston College) 5-11 200 4.54: With three years of starting experience under his belt, Boston College cornerback Kamrin Moore should be a decent Day 3 pick who doesn't need as much schooling as some other players drafted around the same time from his position. The problem with Moore is that he is not overly fast and he struggles when dealing with the deep threat receivers he will see an increased amount of in the NFL.

*Rashaan Gaulden (Tennessee) 6-0 193 4.54: Stay in school man. We don't agree at all with the decision of Tennessee cornerback Rashaan Gaulden to come out early as the position is so stacked with star underclassmen that he figures to slip much further than anticipated. It is not that Gaulden is a bad player but he still could use some seasoning in all facets. What Gaulden has going for him though is a nice combination of size and speed that will attract a large segment of NFL personnel execs. It is likely some team will be seduced by those traits and with the proper coaching, Gaulden could bear some nice results.

Issac Yiadom (Boston College) 6-1 190 4.58: Boston College cornerback Issac Yiadom may have to move over to safety to make it in the NFL as he is a bit too slow of foot to keep up with the quicker wideouts he would have to deal with on the outside. Yiadom is a physical player who does a nice job helping out in the run game but his lack of speed will be exposed if he does stick at cornerback in the pros.

Darius Phillips (Western Michigan) 5-9 190 4.53: When you take a closer look at Western Michigan's Darius Phillips, you can quickly see how his immense physical/athletic ability leads to big plays at a high level on the collegiate side of things. Despite being short for a corner, Phillips makes up for it with terrific speed and the ability to make plays on the football through excellent leaping ability and good hand technique in coverage. Phillips is also a tremendous return guy who can help there right off the bat. Playing the outside in the NFL is likely not in the cards but it wouldn't surprise us if he bucked this line of thinking.

THE REST

D'Montre Wade (Murray State) 6-0 200 4.56:

Brandon Facyson (Virginia Tech) 6-2 191 4.52

Michael Joseph (Dubuque) 6-1 180 4.55:

Jordan Thomas (Oklahoma) 6-0 192 4.52

Deatrick Nichols (South Florida) 5-10 189 4.53

Andre Chachere (San Jose State) 6-0 200 4.40

Nik Needham (UTEP) 6-0 190 4.59:

Donovan Wilson (Texas A @ M) 6-1 205 4.55

Ranthony Texada (TCU) 5-10 170 4.51

KICKERS

1. Daniel Carlson (Auburn)

2. Eddy Pineiro (Florida)

3. Michael Badgley (Miami Fla.)

PUNTERS

1. Michael Dickson (Texas)

2. Johnny Townsend (Florida)

3. JK Scott (Alabama)

4. Will Gleeson (Ole Miss)

5. Trevor Daniel (Tennessee)

2018 NFL DRAFT ROUND 1 LOG

1. CLEVELAND-

2. NY GIANTS-

3. INDIANAPOLIS-

4. CLEVELAND-

5. DENVER-

6. NY JETS-

7. TAMPA BAY-

8. CHICAGO-

9. SAN FRANCISCO-

10. OAKLAND-

11. MIAMI-

12. CINCINNATI-

13. WASHINGTON-

14. GREEN BAY-

15. ARIZONA-

16. BALTIMORE-

17. LOS ANGELES CHARGERS-

18. SEATTLE-

19. DALLAS-

20. DETROIT-

21. BUFFALO-

22. BUFFALO-

23. LOS ANGELES RAMS-

24. CAROLINA-

25. TENNESSEE-

26. ATLANTA-

27. NEW ORLEANS-

28. PITTSBURGH-

29. JACKSONVILLE-

30. PHILADELPHIA-

31. MINNESOTA-

32. NEW ENGLAND-

****LAST FOUR WERE PROJECTED AS WE WENT TO PRESS PRIOR TO AFC AND NFC TITLE GAMES.******

Made in the USA
Middletown, DE
16 April 2018